Pronunciation

Symbols used in this dictionary:

Vowels

a	as in b*a*d, f*a*t
ah	as in f*a*ther, oomp*ah*
aw	as in s*aw*, *aw*ful
ay	as in m*a*ke, h*ay*
e	as in b*e*d, h*ea*d
ee	as in sh*ee*p, k*ey*
eə	as in th*ere*, h*air*
i	as in sh*i*p, l*i*ck
ie	as in b*i*te, l*ie*d
ie·ə	as in f*ire*, l*iar*
iə	as in h*ere*, f*ear*
o	as in p*o*t, cr*o*p
oh	as in n*o*te, J*oa*n
oo	as in p*u*t, c*oo*k
ooh	as in b*oo*t, l*u*te
ooə	as in j*u*ry, c*ure*
ow	as in n*ow*, b*ough*
owə	as in *our*, p*ower*
oy	as in b*oy*, l*oi*ter
oyə	as in empl*oyer*
u	as in c*u*t, l*u*ck
uh	as in b*ir*d, abs*ur*d
ə	as in m*o*ther, *a*bout

Consonants

b	as in *b*ad
ch	as in *ch*eer
d	as in *d*ay
dh	as in *th*ey
f	as in *f*ew
g	as in *g*ay
h	as in *h*ot
j	as in *j*ump
k	as in *k*ing
kh	as in lo*ch*
l	as in *l*ed
m	as in *m*an
n	as in su*n*
ng	as in su*ng*
nh	as in restaura*nt*
p	as in *p*ot
r	as in *r*ed
s	as in *s*oon
sh	as in fi*sh*
t	as in *t*ea
th	as in *th*ing
v	as in *v*iew
w	as in *w*et
y	as in *y*et
z	as in *z*ero
zh	as in plea*s*ure

The pronunciations in this dictionary are concise and easy to understand, since they are based almost entirely on English spelling, and special characters or marks have been largely avoided.

The dictionary attempts to give the most common variant pronunciations of each word or name. The pronunciation represented here is what may be called a 'standard' or 'neutral British English' accent.

All pronunciations are shown within slant lines / /. The symbol /'/ is placed before the syllable with primary stress. For longer words which have secondary stress on another syllable the symbol /,/ is used before that syllable. Alternative stress patterns are shown by using a hyphen to represent each syllable.

A schwa /ə/ is used to represent the unstressed vowel sound in mother, about, purpose, and may correspond to many different vowels in ordinary spelling.

A bracketed schwa /(ə)/ is used when the sound /ə/ may be either pronounced or missed out, or where its presence or absence is uncertain.

A centred dot (·) separates pairs of letters that might otherwise be wrongly read as one sound.

A swung dash (~) means that the plural is pronounced in the same way as the singular.

Longman Top Pocket Series

TOP POCKET

MUSIC
DICTIONARY

WITHDRAWN
FROM STOCK

Longman

780·3

Longman Group Limited,
Longman House, Burnt Mill, Harlow,
Essex CM20 2JE, England
and Associated Companies throughout the world.

© Merriam-Webster Inc. and
Longman Group Limited 1985

First published 1985

British Library Cataloguing in Publication Data
Top pocket dictionary.
 1. Music—Dictionaries
 780'.3'21   ML100

 ISBN 0-582-89210-4

Typeset by Computerset (MFK) Ltd, Ely, Cambridgeshire.

Printed in Great Britain by
Richard Clay (The Chaucer Press) Ltd,
Bungay, Suffolk

Foreword

Here is a handy pocket reference book for all those interested in music.

Extracted from the Longman data base, this pocket-format dictionary presents accurate and up-to-date definitions in a clear, concise, and easy-to-understand manner.

Over 2000 entries cover musical facts and figures to satisfy all enthusiasts – from choristers to cornettists, balletomanes to bell ringers, and promenaders to percussionists.

The dictionary includes biographical information on over 500 composers, conductors, dancers, and instrumentalists; descriptions of nearly 400 musical instruments and equipment; explanations of some 300 directions used in music; and over 200 definitions of musical forms.

Entries have an easy-to-understand guide to their pronunciation – an especially useful inclusion for the technical and foreign vocabulary.

Illustrations appear after the following headwords: **direction, key signature, music, note,** and **time signature**.

Words printed in SMALL CAPITALS denote headwords at which further information can be found.

Abbreviations
used in this dictionary

abbr	abbreviation
adj	adjective
adv	adverb
Br	British
c	century, centuries
cap	capital, capitalized
conj	conjunction
e g	for example
esp	especially
etc	et cetera
imper	imperative
interj	interjection
n	noun
NAm	North American
pl	plural
prep	preposition
pron	pronoun
sing	singular
specif	specifically
usu	usually
vb	verb
vi	verb intransitive
vt	verb transitive

A

a /ay/ *n, pl* **a's, as** *often cap*
the 6th note of a C-major scale

Abbado, Claudio /a'bahdoh/
(born 1933) Italian conductor

absolute pitch *n*
1 the pitch of a note determined by its rate of vibration
2 the ability to sing or name a note asked for or heard

a cappella *also* **a capella** /ˌah kə'pelə/ *adv or adj*
without instrumental accompaniment

accel. *adv or adj*
accelerando

accelerando /əkˌselə'randoh/ *n, adv, or adj*
(a passage that gets) gradually faster

accent /'aksənt/ *n*
1 greater stress given to 1 note
2 a symbol used to indicate stress – see illustration at
DIRECTION – **accent** *vt*, **accentless** *adj*

acciaccatura /əˌchakə'tooərə/ *n*
a discordant note sounded with or before a principal note or
chord and immediately released – see illustration at
DIRECTION

accidental /ˌaksi'dentl/ *n*
(a sign indicating) a note altered to sharp, flat, or natural
and foreign to a key indicated by a key signature – see
illustration at MUSIC

accompaniment /ə'kump(ə)nimənt/ *n*
a subordinate instrumental or vocal part supporting or
complementing a principal voice or instrument

accompany /ə'kump(ə)ni/ *vb*
to perform an accompaniment (to or for) – **accompanist** *n*

accordion /ə'kawdi·ən/ n
a portable keyboard wind instrument in which the wind is
forced past free reeds by means of a hand-operated bellows
– **accordionist** n

acid rock n
rock music marked by long passages of electronic musical
effects intended to convey the atmosphere of drug-induced
hallucinations

acoustic /ə'koohstik/ also **acoustical** /-kl/ adj
of or being an instrument (e g a guitar) whose sound is not
electronically modified – **acoustically** adv

action /'aksh(ə)n/ n
1 a mechanism connecting the keys with the sounding part
(e g strings or pipes) of a keyboard instrument
2 the manner in which a mechanism operates; specif the
response or resistance of keys in a keyboard instrument to
the player's fingers

adage /a'dahzh/ n
1 a series of sustained and perfectly controlled dance
movements (e g ballet exercises) displaying balance and
grace
2 the first movement of the traditional four-part duet or pas
de deux in ballet

adagietto /ə,dahji'etoh/ adv or adj
less slow than adagio

adagio¹ /ə'dahjioh/ adv or adj
in an easy slow graceful manner

adagio² n, pl **adagios**
1 a composition or movement in adagio tempo
2 ballet dancing, esp a pas de deux, involving difficult feats
of balance

adagissimo /ə,dah'jisimoh/ adv or adj
slower than adagio

Adam, Adolphe Charles /'adəm/

(1803–56) French composer of operas, ballets, etc; works include the ballet *Giselle*

Addinsell, Richard /ˈadinˌsel/
(1904–77) English composer of incidental music for plays and films; works include the *Warsaw Concerto*

Adler, Larry /ˈadlə/
(born 1914) American harmonica player

ad lib. *n or adv*
ad libitum

ad libitum /ˌad ˈlibitəm/ *n or adv*
(a passage to be played) in accordance with the player's own wishes

aeolian harp /eeˈohli·ən/ *n*
a stringed instrument on which the wind produces varying harmonics over the same fundamental tone

aeolian mode *n, often cap A*
an authentic mode which may be represented on the white keys of the piano on a scale from A to A

affrettando /ˌafrəˈtandoh/ *adv or adj*
becoming faster or more agitated

agitato /ˌagiˈtahtoh/ *adv or adj*
restless and agitated

air /eə/ *n*
a tune, melody

Albanesi, Licia /olbəˈnayzi/
(born 1913) American (Italian-born) soprano

Albéniz, Isaac /alˈbayneeth/
(1860–1909) Spanish composer and pianist; works include the piano suite *Iberia*

Albinoni, Tomaso /albiˈnohni/
(1671–1751) Italian composer

Alda, Frances /ˈoldə/
née *Frances Davies* (1883–1952) New Zealand-born soprano

aleatoric /ˌali·əˈtorik/ *adj*

an etymological distortion of 'aleatory'

aleatory /'ali·ət(ə)ri/ *adj*
of music in which the composer intends random chance to
be an element

alla breve /ˌalə 'brevi/ *n, adv, or adj*
(a sign marking a piece to be played) in duple or quadruple
time with the beat represented by a minim – see illustration
at DIRECTION

allargando /aˌlah'gandoh/ *adv or adj*
becoming gradually broader

allegretto /ˌali'gretoh/ *n, adv, or adj, pl* **allegrettos**
(a composition or movement to be played) at a speed faster
than andante but not so fast as allegro

Allegri, Gregorio /ə'laygri/
(1582–1652) Italian composer

allegro /ə'legroh/ *n, adv, or adj, pl* **allegros**
(a composition or movement to be played) in a brisk lively
manner

alleluia /ˌali'looh·yə/ *n or interj*
(a shout, song, etc) used to express praise, joy, or thanks

allemande /'aləmand/ *n often cap*
(music for) a 17th- and 18th-c court dance in moderate
duple or quadruple tempo, often the opening movement of
a suite

alphorn /'alpˌhawn/ *n*
a long straight wooden horn used, esp formerly, by Swiss
herdsmen to call sheep and cattle

alto /'altoh/ *n, pl* **altos**
1a a countertenor
1b a contralto
2 the second highest part in 4-part harmony
3 a member of a family of instruments having a range
between the treble or soprano and the tenor – **alto** *adj*

alto clef *n*

a C clef placing middle C on the 3rd line of the staff – see illustration at MUSIC

anacrusis /ˌanəˈkroohsis/ *n, pl* **anacruses** /-ˌseez/
  1 or more notes preceding the first downbeat of a phrase

andante /anˈdanti/ *n, adv, or adj*
  (a composition or movement to be played) moderately slowly, at a walking pace

andantino /ˌandanˈteenoh/ *n, adv, or adj, pl* **andantinos**
  (a composition or movement to be played) rather quicker than andante or somewhat slower than andante

Anderson, Marian /ˈandəˌsən/
  (born 1902) American contralto

Andrews, Julie Elizabeth /ˈandroohz/
  (born 1935) English actress and singer

Angeles, Victoria de los /ˈangaylayz/
  (born 1923) Spanish soprano

anglaise /ongˈglayz/ *n*
  (the music for) an old English country dance in simple time, usu part of a suite

Anglican chant /ˈangˈglikən/ *n*
  a harmonized melody used in the Anglican church for singing esp psalms and canticles and based on the Gregorian tones

anima /ˈanimah/ *n*
  soul – usu in *con anima*

animato /ˌaniˈmahtoh/ *adv or adj*
  with liveliness and vigour

answer /ˈahnsə/ *n*
  the imitation or exact transposition of the subject of a fugue by a different part, usu at the interval of a fifth above or a fourth below

anthem /ˈanthəm/ *n*
  1 a short choral work
  2 a song or hymn of praise or gladness

anticipation /anˌtisiˈpaysh(ə)n/ *n*
an effect whereby one or more notes of a chord are heard
before the rest of the harmony is changed

antiphon /ˈantifən, -fon/ *n*
a verse, usu from Scripture, said or sung usu before and
after a canticle, psalm, or psalm verse as part of the liturgy
– **antiphonal** *adj*

antiphonary /anˈtifən(ə)ri/ *also* **antiphonal** /anˈtifənl/ *n*
a book containing antiphons and chants sung at services of
the Divine Office

antiphony /anˈtifəni/ *n*
responsive alternation between 2 groups of performers

anvil /ˈanvil/ *n*
an orchestral percussion instrument, imitating a true anvil,
that consists of steel bars and a striker

a piacere /ˌah pyahˈchayri/ *adv or adj*
at pleasure; ad libitum

appassionato /əˌpasiəˈnahtoh/ *n, adv, or adj, pl*
appassionatos
with passion

appoggiatura /əˌpojəˈtooərə/ *n*
an embellishing note preceding an essential melodic note,
used chiefly in the 18th c – see illustration at DIRECTION

arabesque /ˌarəˈbesk/ *n*
1 a posture in ballet in which the dancer is supported on one
leg with one arm extended forwards and the other arm and
leg backwards
2 a short decorative composition

aria /ˈahri·ə/ *n, pl* **arias**
an accompanied melody sung (e g in an opera) by 1 voice

arietta /ˌariˈeta, ˌahri-/ *n*
a short relatively simple aria

Armstrong, (Daniel) Louis /ˈahmˌstrong/
'Satchmo' (1900–71) American jazz musician

Arne, Thomas Augustine /ahn/
(1710–78) English composer, esp of operas and oratorios

Arnold, Malcolm /'ahnəld/
(born 1921) English composer of orchestral, chamber, and film music

arpeggio /ah'pejioh/ *n, pl* **arpeggios**
(the sounding of) a chord whose notes are played in succession, not simultaneously – see illustration at
DIRECTION

arrange /ə'raynj/ *vt*
to adapt (a composition) by scoring for different voices or instruments – **arranger** *n*

arrangement /-mənt/ *n*
an adaptation of a composition for different voices or instruments

Arrau, Claudio /'arow/
(born 1903) Chilean pianist

Ashkenazy, Vladimir /ashkə'nahzi/
(born 1937) Soviet pianist and conductor

Ashton, Sir Frederick William Mallandaine /'ashtən/
(born 1904) English choreographer

assai /ə'sie/ *adv*
very – used with tempo directions <*allegro* ~>

Astaire, Fred /ə'steə/
né *Frederick Austerlitz* (born 1899) American dancer and actor

a tempo /ˌah 'tempoh/ *adv or adj*
in the original time

atonal /a'tohnl, ay-/ *adj*
1 not tonal
2 organized without reference to a key and using the notes of the chromatic scale impartially – **atonalism** *n*, **atonalist** *n*, **atonally** *adv*, **atonalistic** *adj*, **atonality** *n*

attacca /ə'takə/ *vb imperative*

attack at once – used as a direction at the end of a
movement to begin the next without pause; compare SEGUE

attack /ə'tak/ n
the act or manner of beginning a tone or phrase <*a sharp
~*>

attitude /'atityoohd/ n
a ballet position in which one leg is raised at the back and
bent at the knee

Auber, Daniel-François-Esprit /oh'bea/
(1782–1871) French composer of operatic works

augmentation /ˌawgmen'taysh(ə)n/ n
the treatment of a theme, esp in a fugue, in longer note
values than the original

augmented /awg'mentid/ adj
of an interval made a semitone greater than major or perfect
– compare DIMINISHED, MAJOR, MINOR, PERFECT

Austral, Florence /'ostrəl/
pseudonym of *Florence Wilson* (1894–1968) Australian
soprano

authentic /aw'thentik/ adj
of a church mode ranging upwards an octave from the
keynote – compare PLAGAL

Autoharp /'awtoh,hahp/ trademark
a chord zither with button-controlled dampers

ayre /eə/ n
old spelling of *air*, used for a type of English song

B

b /bee/ *n, pl* **b's, bs** *often cap*
the 7th note of a C-major scale

baby grand *n*
a small grand piano

Bach, Carl Philipp Emanuel /bahk, bahkh/
second son of JS, (1714–88) German composer, esp of keyboard works

Bach, Johann Christian
youngest son of JS, (1735–82) German composer of orchestral works, operas, oratorios, and chamber and piano works

Bach, Johann Sebastian
(1685–1750) German composer and organist; works include numerous cantatas, oratorios, concertos, and chamber and keyboard music

Bach, Wilhelm Friedemann
eldest son of JS, (1710–84) German composer and organist

Backhaus, Wilhelm /'bak,hows/
(1884–1969) German pianist

Baez, Joan /'bie·əz/
(born 1941) American folksinger

bag /bag/ *n*
the air reservoir of a bagpipe, usu made of animal skin and containing holes into which are inserted the stocks for the mouth pipe, the chanter, and the drone

bagatelle /,bagə'tel/ *n*
a short piece in a light style; *esp* a short light piece for piano

bagpipe /'bag,piep/ *n*, **bagpipes** *n taking sing or pl vb*
a wind instrument consisting of a bag, mouth tube, chanter, and drone pipes – **bagpiper** *n*

Bailey, Pearl Mae /'bayli/

(born 1918) American singer

Baillie, Dame Isobel /'bayli/

(1895–1983) Scottish soprano

Baker, Dame Janet Abbott /'baykə/

(born 1933) English mezzo-soprano

Baker, Josephine

(1906–75) American dancer and singer

Balakirev, Mily /bə'lakirev/

(1837–1910) Russian composer, leader of nationalist group 'The Five'

balalaika /ˌbalə'liekə/ n

an instrument of Russian origin, usu having 3 strings and a triangular body which is played by plucking

Balanchine, George /ˌbalən'cheen/

né *Georgy Melitonovich Balanchivadze* (born 1904) American (Russian-born) choreographer

Balfe, Michael William /balf/

(1808–70) Irish composer and singer; works include the opera *The Bohemian Girl*

ballad /'baləd/ n

a (slow, romantic, or sentimental) popular, esp narrative, song – **balladic** adj

ballade /bə'lahd, ba-/ n

1 a composition, usu for piano, in a narrative style

2 a form of French medieval poetry and music

ballad opera n

opera that flourished in England in the late 17th and early 18th c, consisting of spoken dialogue interrupted by simple songs or ballads usu set to popular tunes of the day

ballerina /ˌbalə'reenə/ n

a female, esp principal, ballet dancer

ballerino /ˌbalə'reenoh/ n

a male ballet dancer

ballet /'balay; *NAm also* bə'lay/ n

1 (a group that performs) artistic dancing in which the graceful flowing movements are based on conventional positions and steps
2 a theatrical art form using ballet dancing, music, and scenery to convey a story, theme, or atmosphere – **balletic** *adj*

balletomane /ˈbalitəmayn, bəˈletəmayn/ *n*
a devotee of ballet – **balletomania** *n*

ballroom dancing /ˈbawlroohm, -room/ *n*
a usu formal type of dancing done esp by couples for recreation, exhibition, or competition

band /band/ *n taking sing or pl vb*
a group of musicians organized for ensemble playing and using chiefly woodwind, brass, and percussion instruments – compare ORCHESTRA

bandleader /-ˌleedə/ *n*
the director of a dance band

bandmaster /-ˌmahstə/ *n*
a conductor of an esp military band

bandsman /-mən/ *n*
a member of a band

bandstand /-ˌstand/ *n*
an outdoor stand or platform, usu roofed, on which a band plays

banjo /ˈbanjoh, -ˈ-/ *n, pl* **banjos** *also* **banjoes**
an instrument with a drumlike body and fretted strings that are usu strummed with the fingers – **banjoist** *n*

Bantock, Sir Granville /ˈban,tok/
(1868–1946) English composer esp of choral music

bar /bah/ *n*
1 (a group of notes and rests that add up to a prescribed time value, bounded on each side on the staff by) a bar line – see illustration at MUSIC
2 a barre

Barber, Samuel /ˈbahˌbə/
(1910–81) American composer

barbershop /ˈbahbəˌshop/ *n*
unaccompanied vocal harmonizing of popular songs, esp by
a male quartet

Barbirolli, Sir John /ˌbahbiˈroli/
(1899–1970) English conductor

barcarole , barcarolle /ˌbahkəˈrohl/ *n*
(music imitating) a Venetian boat song usu in or
characterized by the alternation of a strong and a weak beat
in ⁶₈ time that suggests a rowing rhythm

bard /bahd/ *n*
someone, specif a Celtic poet-singer, who composed, sang,
or recited verses on heroes and their deeds – **bardic** *adj*

Barenboim, Daniel /ˈbarənˌboym/
(born 1942) Israeli (Argentine-born) pianist and conductor

baritone /ˈbaritohn/ *n*
1 (a person with) a male singing voice between bass and
tenor
2 a member of a family of instruments having a range next
below that of the tenor – **baritone** *adj*, **baritonal** *adj*

bar line *n*
a vertical line across a staff before the first beat of a bar –
see illustration at MUSIC

barn dance *n*
a type of country dance, esp a round dance or a square
dance with called instructions; *also* a social gathering for
such dances

baroque /bəˈrok/ *adj*
(typical) of a style of art prevalent esp in the 17th c that is
marked by extravagant forms and elaborate and sometimes
grotesque ornamentation – **baroquely** *adv*

barre /bah/ *n*
a horizontal handrail used by ballet dancers while exercising

barrelhouse /'barəl,hows/ *n*
a style of jazz characterized by a heavy beat and simultaneous improvisation by players

barrel organ *n*
an instrument consisting of a revolving cylinder studded with pegs that open a series of valves to admit air from a bellows to a set of pipes

Bart, Lionel /baht/
(born 1930) English composer, lyricist, and dramatist

Bartók, Béla /'bah,tok/
(1881–1945) Hungarian composer; works include several for the stage, choral, chamber, and orchestral music, and many volumes of folk song arrangements

Basie, William /'bayzi/
'Count Basie' (born 1904) American bandleader

bass¹ /bays/ *adj*
1 of low pitch
2 of or having the range or part of a bass

bass² *n*
1a the lowest part in written, sung, or played music; *esp* the lowest part in conventional 4-part harmony
1b the lower half of the whole vocal or instrumental tonal range – compare TREBLE
2 (a person with) the lowest adult male singing voice
3 a member of a family of instruments having the lowest range; *esp* a double bass or bass guitar
4 any of several button keys on an accordion which when depressed sound a single bass note or a chord built on a particular note

bass-bar *n*
an oblong piece of wood attached lengthways to the top or belly within the body of an instrument of the violin class, for withstanding the pressure at the bridge and distributing the vibrations

bass clef *n*
1 a clef placing the F below middle C on the fourth line of the staff
2 the bass staff – called also F CLEF; compare TREBLE CLEF; see illustration at MUSIC

bass drum *n*
a large drum with 2 heads that gives a booming sound of low indefinite pitch

basse danse /ˈbas ˌdahns/ *n*
a stately 15th-c court dance that was precursor of the minuet

basset horn /ˈbasit/ *n*
an early tenor clarinet having a range extending down to F at the bottom of the bass staff

bass guitar *n*
a usu electric guitar with four strings tuned like those of a double bass

bass horn *n*
a wind instrument of the late 18th and early 19th c that is a variety of the serpent having the tube bent back on itself in a single loop rather than being coiled

bassist /ˈbaysist/ *n*
a double bass player

basso /ˈbasoh/ *n, pl* **bassos, bassi** /-si/
an (operatic) bass singer

bassoon /bəˈsoohn/ *n*
1 a double-reed woodwind instrument with a usual range 2 octaves lower than the oboe
2 a 16-foot pipe organ stop imitating the bassoon in tone – **bassoonist** *n*

basso ostinato *n*
an ostinato occurring in the bass

basso profundo /prəˈfoondoh/ *n, pl* **basso profundos**
(a person with) an exceptionally low bass singing voice

bass viol *n*

a viola da gamba

Bate, Stanley /bayt/

(1913–59) English composer and pianist

baton /'bat(ə)n, 'ba₁ton, bə'ton/ *n*

a stick with which the conductor of a band or orchestra beats time and secures expressive playing

Bax, Sir Arnold Edward Trevor /baks/

(1883–1953) English composer

beat[1] /beet/ *vb*

1 *vt* to strike repeatedly in order to produce music or a signal

2 *vt* to indicate by beating

3 *vi* to pulsate, throb

4 *vi* to sound on being struck <*the drums were* ~*ing*>

beat[2] *n*

1 (the rhythmic effect of) a metrical or rhythmic stress

2 the tempo indicated to a performer – **beatless** *adj*

beater /'beetə/ *n*

a stick for beating a gong

bebop /'bee₁bop/ *n*

jazz characterized by unusual dissonant chord structures, syncopated rhythms, harmonic complexity and innovation, and a lengthened and improvised melodic line – **bebopper** *n*

Beecham, Sir Thomas /'bee₁chəm/

(1879–1961) English conductor

Beethoven, Ludwig van /'bay₁tohvən/

(1770–1827) German composer; works include 9 symphonies, the opera *Fidelio*, the *Missa Solemnis* (Mass in D), and several concertos, string quartets, and piano sonatas

beguine /bi'geen/ *n*

a vigorous popular West Indian dance

Beiderbecke, Bix /'biedə₁bek/

(1903–31) American pianist and cornetist

Belafonte, Harry /₁belə'fontay/

(born 1927) American singer and actor

bel canto /ˌbel 'kantoh/ n

operatic singing stressing ease, purity, evenness of tone production, and an agile and precise vocal technique

bell /bel/ n

1 a hollow metallic device, usu cup-shaped with a flaring mouth if operated manually, and saucer-shaped if part of an electrical or clockwork device, that vibrates and gives a ringing sound when struck

2 the flared end of a wind instrument

Bellini, Vincenzo /ˌbəˈleeni/

(1801–35) Italian composer, esp of operas

bell metal n

a bronze with a high tin content, used for making bells

bellows /ˈbelohz/ n taking sing or pl vb

the pleated expandable part of a concertina or accordion that supplies a current of air

belly dance n

a usu solo dance emphasizing movements of the belly – **belly dance** vi, **belly dancer** n

Benedicite /ˌbeniˈdisitay, -tee/ n

(a musical setting of) a hymn of praise to God beginning 'All the works of the Lord, bless ye the Lord'

Benedictus /ˌbeniˈdiktus/ n

1 part of the Sanctus section of the Mass

2 (a musical setting of) the canticle of Zacharias in Luke 1:68 that begins 'Blessed be the Lord God of Israel' and forms part of the services of *Lauds* and *Morning Prayer*

Bennett, Richard Rodney /ˈbenət/

(born 1936) English composer and pianist

berceuse /beəˈsuhz/ n, pl **berceuses** /~/

(a composition in the style of) a lullaby

Berg, Alban /buhg/

(1885–1935) Austrian composer; works include the opera

Wozzeck and the *Chamber Concerto* for violin, piano, and 13 wind instruments

bergamask, bergamasque /ˌbuhgəˈmahsk/ *n*
(the music for) an Italian peasant dance in duple time

Berkeley, Sir Lennox Randal /ˈbahkli/
(born 1903) English composer of operas and piano, chamber, and orchestral music

Berlin, Irving /ˌbuhˈlin/
né *Israel Baline* (born 1888) American (Russian-born) composer of popular songs

Berlioz, (Louis) Hector /ˈbeəliˌohz/
(1803–69) French composer of orchestral and choral music; works include the *Symphonie fantastique*, the opera *Les Troyens*, and the choral piece *L'Enfance du Christ*

Bernstein, Leonard /ˈbuhnˌstien, -ˌsteen/
(born 1918) American conductor and composer

bewegt /bəˈvaykt/ *adv or adj*
agitated

bible regal *n*
a regal which folds into 2 like a book

bichord /ˈbieˌkawd/ *n*
any of the paired strings of a piano that produce the notes in the middle range – compare TRICHORD

binary /ˈbienəri/ *adj*
having 2 subjects or 2 complementary sections <~ *form*> –
binary *n*

bind /biend/ *n*
a tie – see illustration at DIRECTION

bis /bis/ *adv*
again, twice – used to direct repetition of a passage or to request an encore

Bizet, Alexandre César Léopold /ˈbee,zay/
'Georges' (1838–75) French composer of operas, best known of which is *Carmen*, orchestral suites and overtures,

17

piano pieces, and songs

black bottom *n, often cap both Bs*

an American dance popular from 1926 to 1928, with sinuous movements of the hips and rocking steps – **black-bottom** *vb*

blast /blahst/ *n*

the sound produced by air blown through a wind instrument or whistle

Bliss, Sir Arthur /blis/

(1891–1975) English composer

Bloch, Ernest /blok/

(1880–1959) American (Swiss-born) composer of orchestral, chamber, and choral works

block /blok/ *n*

1 a wooden percussion instrument played by striking with a drumstick or mallet

2 (a ballet shoe with) a solid toe on which a dancer can stand on points

blow /bloh/ *vb*

1 *vi* to send forth a current of air

2 *vi* to make a sound by blowing

3 *vt* to act on with a current of air

blowhole, blow hole *n*

the opening at the upper end of a wind instrument (e g a flute) without a specialized mouthpiece. Air blown into the blowhole vibrates after being directed against a sharp edge.

Blow, John /bloh/

(1649–1708) English composer and organist

bluegrass /'blooh,grahs/ *n*

a type of country music played on unamplified stringed instruments

blue note *n*

a flattened note, usu a third or seventh, used esp in jazz and blues in a chord where a major interval would be expected

blues /bloohz/ *n, pl* **blues**

(a song in) a melancholy style in quadruple time characterized by 12-bar phrases, 3-line stanzas, and the occurrence of blue notes in the melody and harmony *<singing the ~>* – **bluesy** *adj*

bob /bob/ *n*
(a method of bell ringing using) a modification of the order in change ringing

Boccherini, Luigi /ˌbokəˈreeni/
(1743–1805) Italian cellist and composer of esp chamber music

body /ˈbodi/ *n*
the sound box or pipe of a musical instrument

Boehm, Theobald /buhm/
(1794–1881) German flautist and inventor who made several fundamental improvements to the instrument

bolero /bəˈleəroh/ *n, pl* **boleros**
(music for) a lively Spanish dance, characterized by sharp turns, stamping, and sudden pauses in a position with one arm arched over the head

bones /bohnz/ *n pl*
thin bars of bone, ivory, or wood held in pairs between the fingers and used to produce musical rhythms

bongo /ˈbong·goh/ *n, pl* **bongos** *also* **bongoes**
a small tuned drum, usu played in 2s or 3s with the hands – **bongoist** *n*

boogie /ˈboohgi/ *n*
boogie-woogie

boogie-woogie /ˈwoohgi/ *n*
a percussive style of playing blues on the piano characterized by a steady rhythmic 12-bar ground bass in quadruple time and a simple, often improvised, melody

bop¹ /bop/ *n*
bebop – **bopper** *n*

bop² *vi*

to dance (e g in a disco) in a casual and unrestricted
manner, esp to popular music

Borodin, Alexander Porfirevich /ˌborəˈdin/
(1833–87) Russian composer and chemist; works include the
opera *Prince Igor*

bossa nova /ˌbosə ˈnohvə/ *n*
(music for) a Brazilian dance similar to the samba

bottleneck /ˈbotlˌnek/ *n*
a style of guitar playing using an object (e g a metal bar or
the neck of a bottle) pressed against the strings to produce
the effect of one note sliding into another

Boulanger, Nadia Juliette /ˈboolonhˌzhay/
(born 1887) French composer and teacher

Boulez, Pierre /booˈlez/
(born 1925) French composer, conductor, and pianist

Boult, Sir Adrian Cedric /bohlt/
(1889–1983) English conductor

bourdon /ˈbooədn, ˈbawdn/ *n*
1 a 16-foot pipe organ stop that produces low notes
2 the 1 of the usu 3 drones of a bagpipe that produces low
notes

bourreé /ˈbooray/ *n*
a 17th-c French dance usu in duple time

bouzouki *also* **bousouki** /booˈzoohki/ *n*
a long-necked Greek stringed instrument that resembles a
mandolin

bow¹ /boh/ *n*
(a stroke made with) a resilient wooden rod with horsehairs
stretched from end to end, used in playing a stringed
instrument

bow² *vb*
to play (a stringed instrument) with a bow

bow hair, hair *n*
the horsehairs of a bow used in playing a stringed

instrument

Boyce, William /boys/
(1711–79) English composer

brace /brays/ *n*
(a mark { or } connecting) 2 or more staves the parts of which are to be performed simultaneously – see illustration at MUSIC

Brahms, Johannes /brahmz/
(1833–97) German composer of 4 symphonies, concertos, chamber and piano music, many songs, and choral works (e g the *German Requiem*)

Brain, Aubrey Harold /brayn/
(1893–1955) English horn player

Brain, Dennis
son of preceding, (1921–57) English horn player

branle *also* **bransle** /'branl/ *n*
1 any of several couple dances of French origin that were popular in the 16th and 17th c
2 a sideways balance step used in branle dances

brass /brahs/ *n taking sing or pl vb*
brass instruments – **brass** *adj*

brass band *n*
a band consisting of brass and percussion instruments

brass instrument *n*
any of a group of wind instruments with a long usu curved cylindrical or conical metal tube, a mouthpiece against which the player's lips vibrate, and usu valves or a slide for producing the notes

bravura /brə'v(y)ooərə/ *n*
a flamboyant brilliant style

break¹ /brayk/ *vi*
of a voice to alter sharply in tone, pitch, or intensity; *esp* to shift abruptly from one register to another <*boys' voices ~ at puberty*>

break² *n*
  1 the point where one register changes to another
  2 a short solo passage, usu improvised, inserted between
  phrases in jazz
Bream, Julian Alexander /breem/
  (born 1933) English guitarist
breathy /'brethi/ *adj*
  characterized or accompanied by the audible passage of
  breath – **breathily** *adv*, **breathiness** *n*
breit /briet/ *adv or adj*
  in a broad manner
Brendel, Alfred /'brendl/
  (born 1931) Austrian pianist
breve /breev/ *n*
  a note equal in time value to 2 semibreves or 4 minims – see
  illustration at NOTE
Brian, (William) Havergal /'brie·ən/
  (1876–1972) English composer
bridge /brij/ *n*
  an arch serving to raise the strings of a musical instrument
Bridge, Frank /brij/
  (1879–1941) English composer, viola player, and conductor
bridge passage *n*
  a passage linking one theme with another
brillante /bri'lantay/ *adv or adj*
  in a showy and sparkling style
brio /'bree·oh/ *n*
  enthusiastic vigour; vivacity, verve – esp in *con brio*
Britten, (Edward) Benjamin /'britən/
  Baron Britten of Aldeburgh (1913–76) English composer,
  conductor, and pianist. Founded the Aldeburgh Festival in
  1948. Works include many operas (e g *Peter Grimes* and
  Billy Budd), choral works, song cycles and songs, and
  chamber and orchestral works (e g *Young Person's Guide to*

the Orchestra).

Broadwood, John /ˈbrawd͵wood/
(1732–1812) Scottish piano maker; founder of firm of piano manufacturers which survives to the present day

Bruch, Max /brook/
(1838–1920) German composer

Bruckner, Anton /ˈbrooknə/
(1824–96) Austrian composer; works include 9 symphonies and choral and chamber music

buffo /ˈboofoh/ *n, pl* **buffi** /ˈboofi/, **buffos**
a male singer of comic roles in opera; a buffoon

bugle[1] /ˈbyoohgl/ *n*
a valveless brass instrument used esp for military calls

bugle[2] *vi*
to sound a bugle – **bugler** *n*

Bull, Ole Bornemann /bool/
(1810–80) Norwegian violinist

Bülow, Hans Guido von /ˈbooh͵loh/
(1830–94) German pianist, conductor, and composer

burden /ˈbuhd(ə)n/ *n*
a chorus, refrain

Bush, Alan Dudley /boosh/
(born 1900) English composer, conductor, and pianist

busk /busk/ *vi*
chiefly Br to sing or play a musical instrument in the street (e g outside a theatre) to earn money – **busker** *n*

Busoni, Ferruccio Benvenuto /b(y)oohˈsohni/
(1866–1924) Italian composer and pianist; works include 4 operas, orchestral and chamber music, and songs

butt /but/ *n*
the 3rd and end joint of a bassoon

Butt, Dame Clara /but/
(1872–1936) English contralto

Butterworth, George Sainton Kaye /ˈbutə͵wuhth/

(1885–1916) English composer

button /'bʌt(ə)n/ *n*
a small knob at the end of a violin or other stringed
instrument, that bears the pull of the strings

button key *n*
a small circular button-shaped key on a concertina,
accordion, or similar instrument

Buxtehude, Dietrich /ˌbʊkstəˈhoohdə/
(1637?–1707) Danish composer and organist

Byrd, William /buhd/
(1543–1623) English composer, esp of church and chamber
music

C

c /see/ *n, pl* **c's, cs** *often cap*
the keynote of a C-major scale

cabaletta /ˌkabəˈletə/ *n*
1 a short aria in popular style characterized by a simple and much reiterated rhythm
2 a fast concluding section of an aria or ensemble

cachucha /kəˈchoohchə/ *n*
a lively Andalusian solo dance in triple time, performed with castanets

cacophony /kəˈkofəni/ *n*
harsh or discordant sound; dissonance – **cacophonous** *adj*

cadence /ˈkayd(ə)ns/ , **cadency** /-si/ *n*
a concluding strain; *specif* a chord sequence moving to a harmonic close or point of rest and giving the sense of harmonic completion – **cadenced** *adj*, **cadential** *adj*

cadenza /kəˈdenzə/ *n*
a showy sometimes improvised solo passage in a concerto

Cage, John Milton /kayj/
(born 1912) American composer and pianist; works feature the inclusion of novel sound effects, esp those produced on his specially invented 'prepared' piano

calando /kəˈlandoh/ *adv or adj*
dying away

calinda /kəˈlində/ *n*
a ceremonial dance of the West Indies and the USA

call¹ /kawl/ *vt*
to give the calls for (a square dance) – **caller** *n*

call² *n*
a summons or signal on a drum, bugle, or pipe

Callas, Maria /ˈkaləs/
(1923–77) American soprano

calypso /kəˈlipsoh/ *n, pl* **calypsos** *also* **calypsoes**
an improvised ballad, usu satirizing current events, in a style
originating in the West Indies – **calypsonian** *n or adj*

campanology /ˌkampəˈnoləji/ *n*
1 the study of bells
2 the art of bell ringing – **campanologist** *n*

Campion, Thomas /ˈkampi·ən/
(1567–1620) English poet and musician

Campoli, Alfredo /kamˈpohli/
(born 1906) British (Italian-born) violinist

canary /kəˈneəri/ *n*
a lively court dance of the 16th c that resembles the gigue

cancan /ˈkanˌkan/ *n*
a French dance performed by women, characterized by high
kicking usu while holding up the front of a full ruffled skirt

canon /ˈkanən/ *n*
a composition for 2 or more voices or instruments in which
the melody is repeated by the successively entering
performers

cantabile[1] /kanˈtahbili, -lay/ *adv or adj*
in a singing manner; melodious, flowing

cantabile[2] *n*
1 cantabile style – used esp of instrumental music in
distinction from recitative or parlando or from the marked
rhythm of dance music
2 a piece or passage in cantabile style

cantando /kanˈtandoh/ *adv or adj*
cantabile

cantata /kanˈtahtə/ *n*
a choral composition comprising choruses, solos, recitatives,
interludes, and orchestral accompaniment

canticle /ˈkantikl/ *n*
a Bible hymn other than a psalm

cantilena /ˌkantiˈlaynə/ *n*

1 (a performance of) a smoothly flowing passage of melody
2 a short song or aria of lyrical character; *also* a solo instrumental passage in this style

cantor /ˈkantaw/ *n*
a singer who leads liturgical music (e g in a synagogue)

cantus firmus /ˌkantəs ˈfiəməs, ˈfuhməs/ , **canto firmo** /ˌkantoh ˈfiəmoh, ˈfuhmoh/ *n, pl* **canti firmi** /ˌkanti ˈfiəmi, ˈfuhmi/
1 a plainchant or simple Gregorian melody, originally sung in unison and prescribed as to form and use by ecclesiastical tradition
2 a melodic theme or subject; *esp* one for contrapuntal treatment

canzona /kanˈtsohnə/ , **canzone** /kanˈtsohni/ *n, pl* **canzoni** /-ni/ *also* **canzones** /-neez/
1 a short instrumental piece
2 a polyphonic setting of a medieval Provençal or Italian lyric poem; *broadly* such a work resembling a madrigal

canzonet /ˌkanzəˈnet/ *also* **canzonetta** /ˌkanzəˈnetə/ *n*
1 a partsong resembling but less elaborate than a madrigal
2 a light and graceful song

capo /ˈkapoh, ˈkay-/ , **capotasto** /-ˈtastoh/ *n, pl* **capos, capotastos**
a movable bar attached to the fingerboard esp of a guitar to raise the pitch of the strings

capriccio /kəˈprichioh/ *n, pl* **capriccios**
an instrumental piece in free form, usu lively in tempo

Cardus, Sir Neville /ˈkahdus/
(1889–1975) English writer on music and cricket

carillon /kəˈrilyən/ *n*
a set of bells sounded by hammers controlled from a manual or pedal keyboard – **carillonneur** *n*

carioca /ˌkariˈohkə/ *n*
(the music for) a dance resembling the samba

Carmichael, Hoagy /'kah‚miekl/
(1899–1981) American composer of popular songs

carol[1] /'karəl/ n
a popular seasonal usu religious song or ballad; *esp* a Christmas song or hymn

carol[2] vb **-ll-** (*NAm* **-l-, -ll-**)
to sing (joyfully)

carry /'kari/ vt
to sing with reasonable correctness of pitch <~ *a tune*>

Carte, Richard D'Oyly /kaht/
(1844–1901) English opera impresario

cartellone /‚kahte'lohni/ n
a list of operas that a company plans to perform during a season

Caruso, Enrico /‚kə'roohsoh/
originally **Errico** (1873–1921) Italian tenor

Casals, Pablo /kə'sahlz/
(1876–1973) Spanish cellist, conductor, and composer

castanets /‚kastə'net/ n
small usu wooden or plastic shells clicked together in the hand and used esp by dancers

castrato /ka'strahtoh/ n, pl **castrati** /-ti/
a singer castrated in boyhood to preserve the high range of his voice

catch /kach/ n
an often humorous or coarse round for 3 or more voices

catgut /'kat‚gut/ n
a tough cord usu made from sheep intestines and used for the strings of musical instruments

Cavalli, Pietro /kə'vali/
(1602–76) Italian composer, esp of operas

cavatina /‚kavə'teenə/ n
1 a short simple operatic solo
2 an instrumental composition in a similar style, usu having

a slow tempo

C clef /see/ *n*

a movable clef indicating middle C by its placement on 1 of
the lines of the staff – compare ALTO CLEF, TENOR CLEF;
see illustration at MUSIC

cebell /sə'bel/ *n*

an old English dance similar to the gavotte

ceilidh /'kayli/ *n*

an informal party for esp Scottish or Irish dancing and music

celesta /sə'lestə/ *n*

a keyboard instrument with hammers that strike steel plates
producing a tone like that of a glockenspiel

celeste /sə'lest/ *n*

a celesta

cello /'cheloh/ *n, pl* **cellos**

abbreviation of *violoncello*: a large stringed instrument of
the violin family tuned an octave below the viola and played
held between the knees, supported on the ground by an
adjustable metal spike – **cellist** *n*

cembalo /'chembə,loh/ *n, pl* **cembali** /-li/, **cembalos**

a harpsichord

Chabrier, (Alexis) Emmanuel /'shabri,ay/

(1841–94) French composer; works include the orchestral
rhapsody *España*

cha-cha /'chah ,chah/ , **cha-cha-cha** *n*

a fast rhythmic ballroom dance of Latin American origin –
cha-cha *vi*

chaconne /shə'kon/ *n*

1 an old Spanish dance tune resembling the passacaglia
2 a composition typically consisting of variations on a
repeated succession of chords

Chaliapin, Feodor Ivanovich /shal'yahpin/

(1873–1938) Russian bass

chamber music *n*

music written for a small group of instruments

chamber orchestra *n*
a small orchestra, usu with 1 player for each instrumental part

change¹ /chaynj/ *vi,*
of the (male) voice to shift to a lower register; break

change² *n*
an order in which a set of bells is struck in change ringing

change ringing *n*
the practice of ringing a set of tuned (church) bells in continually varying order

chanson /'shans(ə)n/ *n, pl* **chansons** /'shans(ə)nz/
a type of French polyphonic song of the 14th to 17th century

chant¹ /chahnt/ *vb*
1 *vi* to sing a chant
2 *vt* to utter as in chanting

chant² *n*
(the music or performance of) a repetitive melody used for liturgical singing in which as many syllables are assigned to each note as required

chanter /'chahntə/ *n*
the reed pipe of a bagpipe with finger holes on which the melody is played

chanteuse /,shan'tuhz, ,shon-/ *n, pl* **chanteuses** /~/
a female (nightclub or cabaret) singer

chanty /'shanti/ *n*
a shanty

Charleston /'chahlstən/ *vi or n*
(to dance) a lively ballroom dance in which the heels are swung sharply outwards on each step

chassé /'shasay/ *vi or n*
(to make) a dance step, esp in ballet, in which a slide on one foot is followed closely by a slide on the other foot in a rhythm resembling that of the gallop

Cherkassky, Shura /ˌchuh'kaski/
(born 1911) Russian-born pianist

Cherubini, Mario Luigi Carlo Zenobia Salvatore
/ˌkayrooh'beeni/
(1760–1842) Italian composer, esp of opera and church music

chest of viols n taking sing or pl vb
a set of usu 6 viols of different sizes for ensemble playing

Chevalier, Albert /shə'val,yay/
(1862–1923) English music-hall entertainer

chime¹ /chiem/ n
1 a musically tuned set of bells
2 a set of objects (e g hanging metal bars or tubes) that sound like bells when struck
3 **chimes** pl, **chime** the sound of a set of bells
4 a musical sound like that of bells

chime² vb
1 vi to make a musical, esp a harmonious, sound
2 vi to make the sounds of a chime
3 vt to cause to chime – **chimer** n

chiming /'chieming/ n
a gentle method of sounding church bells that is used for announcing the hour of the day and in which the bell is usu struck either by an external hammer or by a mechanical movement of the clapper – compare RINGING

chimney /'chimni/ n
a small tube through the top of a stopped metal pipe of an organ, permitting air to escape to sharpen the pitch

chitarrone /ˌkeetə'rohni/ n
a bass or contrabass of the lute family

choir /kwie·ə/ n taking sing or pl vb
an organized company of singers

choirboy /-ˌboy/ n
a boy singer in a choir

choir organ *n*
a division of an organ having mostly soft stops

Chopin, Frédéric François /'shoh,pan/
(1810–49) Polish pianist and composer; works, almost
exclusively for the piano, include numerous études,
mazurkas, nocturnes, and preludes

choral /'kawrəl/ *adj*
accompanied with or designed for singing (by a choir) –
chorally *adv*

chorale *also* **choral** /ko'rahl/ *n*
1 (music composed for) a usu German traditional hymn or
psalm for singing in church
2 *taking sing or pl vb* a chorus, choir

choral symphony *n*
1 a symphony that includes sections of choral music
2 a combined work for orchestra and chorus
3 a usu large work for chorus only

chord¹ /kawd/ *n*
a combination of notes sounded together

chord² *vt*
to add notes to (a melody) to form chords; harmonize

chordal /'kawdl/ *adj*
relating to music characterized more by harmony than
counterpoint

chord organ *n*
an electronic or reed organ with buttons to produce simple
chords

choreograph /'koriə,grahf, -,graf/ *vb*
to compose or arrange the steps and dances for (a ballet or
piece of music) – **choreographer** *n*

choreography /,kori'ogrəfi/ *n*
1 the art of representing dance steps and sequences in
symbols
2 stage dancing as distinguished from social or ballroom

dancing

3 the composition and arrangement of a ballet or other dance for the stage – **choreographic** *adj*, **choreographically** *adv*

chorister /'koristə/ *n*

a singer in a choir; *specif* a choirboy

chorus /'kawrəs/ *n*

1 *taking sing or pl vb*

1a an organized company of singers who sing in concert; *specif* a body of singers who sing the choral parts of a work (e g in opera)

1b a group of dancers and singers supporting the featured players in a musical or revue

2a a part of a song or hymn recurring at intervals

2b a composition sung by a chorus

chromatic¹ /kroh'matik/ *adj*

1 of or giving all the notes of the chromatic scale

2 characterized by frequent use of intervals or notes outside the diatonic scale – **chromatically** *adv*, **chromaticism** *n*

chromatic² *n*

a chromatically altered note; an accidental

chromatic scale *n*

a scale consisting entirely of semitones

church mode *n*

any of several modes prevalent in medieval music

cithara /'sithərə, 'ki-/ *n*

an ancient Greek stringed instrument of the lyre family with a wooden sounding board

cithern /'sidhuhn/ *n*

a cittern

cittern /'sitən/ *n*

a plucked stringed instrument popular esp in Renaissance England

Civil, Alan /'sivl/

(born 1929) English horn player and composer

clapper /'klapə/ *n*
the tongue of a bell

claque /klak/ *n*
a group of people hired to applaud at a performance (e g of an opera)

claqueur /ˌkla'kuh/ *n*
a member of a claque

clarinet /ˌklari'net/ *n*
1 a single-reed woodwind instrument with a usual range from D below middle C upwards for 3 octaves
2 a usu 8-foot reed organ stop with a clarinetlike tone – **clarinettist**, *NAm chiefly* **clarinetist** *n*

clarion /'klari·ən/ *n*
(the sound of) a medieval trumpet

Clarke, Jeremiah /klahk/
(1674–1707) English organist and composer; works include the *Trumpet Voluntary*

classical /'klasikl/ *adj*
1 of or being (a composer of) music of the late 18th c and early 19th c characterized by an emphasis on simplicity, objectivity, and proportion
2 of or being music in the European art tradition that includes such forms as chamber music, opera, and symphony as distinguished from folk, popular music, or jazz

clavichord /'klavi,kawd/ *n*
an early usu rectangular keyboard instrument in which the strings are struck by metal tangents – **clavichordist** *n*

clavier, klavier /'klavi·ə/ *n*
a usu unspecified keyboard instrument – **clavierist** *n*

clef /klef/ *n*
a sign placed on a staff to indicate the pitch represented by the notes following it – see illustration at MUSIC

Clementi, Muzio /ˌkle'menti/

(1752–1832) Italian composer and pianist

cluster /'klustə/
– see TONE CLUSTER

Coates, Eric /kohts/
(1886–1957) English composer and viola player

coda /'kohdə/ *n*
1 a concluding section that is formally distinct from the main structure
2 a symbol indicating a coda – see illustration at DIRECTION

codetta /koh'detə/ *n*
1 a short coda
2 a passage connecting the parts of a movement or the entries in a fugue

col /kohl/ , **coll'**, **colla** /'kohlə/, **colle** /'kohlay/ *prep*
with (the) – usu in combination <~ *legno*>

coll'arco, col arco /ahkoh/ *adv*
with the bow – compare PIZZICATO

Cole, Nat King /kohl/
(1919–65) American singer and pianist

Coleridge-Taylor, Samuel /'kohl(ə),rij 'taylə/
(1875–1912) English composer, esp of choral works (e g *Hiawatha's Wedding Feast*)

colla parte /pahtay/ *adv or adj*
with the solo part in tempo and phrasing – used to direct an accompaniment

colla voce /'voh,chay/ *adv or adj*
colla parte

col legno /koh'laynyoh/ *adv or adj*
with the wood – used to direct players of bowed instruments to use the wood and not the hair of the bow

coloratura /,kolərə'tyooərə/ *n*
elaborate embellishment esp in vocal music

combo /'komboh/ *n, pl* **combos**
a usu small jazz or dance band

come /'koh,may/ *adv*
(in the same manner) as <~ *prima*>

come prima *adv or adj*
in the same manner as the first time

come sopra /sohprə/ *adv or adj*
as previously

common chord *n*
a triad

common time *n*
the metre marked by 4 crotchets per bar

comodo, commodo /'komə,doh/ *adv or adj*
in an easy or convenient tempo

company /'kump(ə)ni/ *n*
an organization of musical or dramatic performers

compass /'kumpəs/ *n*
the range of a voice or instrument from its highest
attainable note to the lowest

compose /kəm'pohz/ *vt*
to formulate and write (a piece of music)

composer /kəm'pohzə/ *n*
a person who writes music

composition /,kompə'zish(ə)n/ *n*
1 the art of creating music
2 a written piece of music, esp of considerable size and
complexity – **compositional** *adj*, **compositionally** *adv*

compound time *n*
a metre (e g ⅜) in which each beat in a bar is divisible into
three, six, etc – see illustration at TIME SIGNATURE

con /kon/ *prep*
with <~ *sordini*>

concert /'konsət, -suht/ *n*
a public performance of music or dancing; *esp* a
performance, usu by a group of musicians, that is made up
of several individual compositions

concertante /ˌkon(t)sə'tantay, ˌkonchə-, -tantə/ *adj*
in a concerted form, used to designate music with a
contrasting element usu with parts for solo instruments or
for several solo instruments without orchestra – compare
CONCERTO GROSSO

concerted /kən'suhtid/ *adj*
arranged in parts for several voices or instruments –
concertedly *adv*, **concertedness** *n*

concert grand /'konsət/ *n*
a grand piano of the largest size for concerts

concertina /ˌkonsə'teenə/ *n*
a small hexagonal instrument of the accordion family

concertino /ˌkonchə'teenoh/ *n, pl* **concertinos**
a short concerto

concertmaster /'konsət,mahstə/ *n*
chiefly NAm LEADER 1

concerto /kən'cheətoh, -'chuh-/ *n, pl* **concerti** /-ti/, **concertos**
a piece for 1 or more soloists and orchestra, usu with 3
movements

concerto grosso /'grosoh/ *n, pl* **concerti grossi** /'grosi/
a piece for a small group of solo instruments and full
orchestra

concert pitch *n*
a tuning standard of usu 440 hertz for A above middle C

concord /'kongkawd, 'kon-/ *n*
a harmonious combination of simultaneously heard notes

concrete music /'kongkreet, 'kon-/ *n*
musique concrète

conduct /kən'dukt/ *vb*
1 *vt* to direct the performance or execution of (a musical
work or group of musicians)
2 *vi* to act as leader or director of an orchestra

conductor /kən'duktə/ *n*
one who directs the performance of musicians –

conga

conductorial *adj*

conga /'kong·gə/ *n*
1 a dance involving 3 steps followed by a kick and performed by a group, usu in single file
2 a tall narrow bass drum beaten with the hands

conservatoire /kən'suhvətwah/, **conservatory** /-t(ə)ri/ *n*
a music school

console /'konsohl, 'konsl/ *n*
the desk containing the keyboards, stops, etc of an organ

consonance /'kons(ə)nəns/ *n*
an agreeable combination of notes in harmony

consonant /'kons(ə)nənt/ *adj*
marked by consonances – **consonantly** *adv*

con sordino, con sordini *adv or adj*
with the mute(s)

consort /'konsawt/ *n*
1 a group of musicians performing esp early music
2 a set of instruments (e g viols or recorders) of the same family played together

continuo /kən'tinyoo,oh/ *n, pl* **continuos**
a part for a keyboard or stringed instrument written as a succession of bass notes with figures that indicate the required chords; *also* (the instruments playing) a continuo accompaniment

contra- /kontrə-/ *prefix*
pitched below normal <contra*bass*>

contrabass¹ /-'bays/ *n*
a double bass

contrabass² *adj*
pitched an octave below the normal bass range

contrabassoon /-bə'soohn/ *n*
a double-reed woodwind instrument having a range an octave lower than that of the bassoon

contralto /kən'traltoh, kən'trahltoh/ *n, pl* **contraltos**

1 (a person with) the lowest female singing voice

2 the part sung by a contralto

contrapuntal /ˌkontrəˈpuntl/ *adj*

of counterpoint – **contrapuntally** *adv*

contredanse /ˈkontrəˌdahns/ , **contradanza** /ˈkontrəˌdantsə/ *n*

(a piece of music for) a folk dance in which couples face each other in 2 lines or in a square

cool /koohl/ *adj*

of or being an understated, restrained, and melodic style of jazz – compare HOT

Copland, Aaron /ˈkohpˌlənd/

(born 1900) American composer, conductor, pianist, and writer

cor anglais /ˌkawr ˈongˈglay ,- -ˈ-/ *n*

a double-reed woodwind instrument similar to, and with a range a fifth lower than, the oboe; also known as English horn

corda /ˈkawdə/ *n*

a string – compare TRE CORDE, UNA CORDA

Corelli, Arcangelo /kəˈreli/

(1653–1713) Italian violinist and composer

cornet /ˈkawnit/ *n*

a valved brass instrument resembling a trumpet but with a shorter tube and less brilliant tone – **cornettist, cornetist** *n*

cornett /kawˈnet/ *n*

a Renaissance woodwind instrument having a cup-shaped mouthpiece like a trumpet and a tapered tube with finger holes like a recorder

coronach /ˈkorənəkh, -nək/ *n*

a Scottish or Irish funeral dirge

corps de ballet /ˌkaw də ˈbalay; *NAm* baˈlay/ *n, pl* **corps de ballet** /~/

the ensemble of a ballet company

corrente /kə'rentay, kaw-/ n

(the music for) an Italian dance in regular triple time that is similar to but faster than the courante

Cortot, Alfred /'kawtoh/

(1877–1962) French pianist and conductor

coryphée /,kori'fay/ n

a ballet dancer who dances in a small group instead of in the corps de ballet or as a soloist

cotillion also **cotillon** /kə'tilyən/ n

an elaborate French dance with frequent changing of partners

counter-exposition n

a second exposition in a fugue, immediately following the first but with the parts entering in a different order

counterpoint /'kowntə,poynt/ n

1 one or more independent melodies added above or below a given melody

2 the combination of 2 or more independent melodies into a single harmonic texture; polyphony

counter-subject n

a contrasting or secondary melody in contrapuntal music

countertenor /'kowntə,tenə/ n

(a person with) an adult male singing voice higher than tenor

country /'kuntri/ n

country music

country and western n

country music

country dance n

any of various native or folk dances for several pairs of dancers typically arranged in square or circular figures or in 2 long rows facing a partner

country music n

music derived from or imitating the folk style of the

southern USA or the western cowboy

coupé /'koohpay/ *n*

a chassé finishing with the displaced foot going into the air

Couperin, François /'koohpə,ranh/

(1668–1733) French organist and composer, esp of keyboard works

coupler /'kuplə/ *n*

a device on a keyboard instrument by which keyboards or keys are connected to play together

couplet /'kuplit/ *n*

a duplet

courante /kooh'rahn(h)t/ *n*

1 a dance of Italian origin consisting of quick running steps
2 a composition or movement (e g in a suite) in quick triple time or in a mixture of $\frac{3}{2}$ and $\frac{6}{4}$ time

Cowell, Henry Dixon /'kow(ə)l/

(1897–1965) American composer, pianist, and writer

cracovienne /krə,kohvee'en/ *n*

a Polish usu group folk dance that combines elements of the ancient round dance, the more recent square dance, and the modern polka

cresc. *adv or adj*

crescendo

crescendo[1] /krə'shendoh/ *n, pl* **crescendos, crescendoes**

1 a gradual increase in volume in a passage
2 a crescendo passage – see illustration at DIRECTION –
crescendo *vi*

crescendo[2] *adv or adj*

with an increase in volume – see illustration at DIRECTION

Cristofori, Bartolomeo /,kristo'fawri/

(1655–1731) Italian inventor of the piano

crook /'krook/ *n*

1 a curved piece of tubing inserted into a wind instrument between the mouthpiece and the body to increase the

number of available pitches. Modern instruments (e g the
French horn) have fixed crooks and the pitch is varied by
means of valves.
2 a curved or hook-shaped tube carrying the mouthpiece of
a recorder, bassoon, or similar instrument

croon /kroohn/ *vb*
to sing usu sentimental popular songs in a low or soft voice
– **croon** *n*, **crooner** *n*

Crosby, Harry Lillis /'krozbi/
'*Bing*' (1904–77) American singer and film actor

Cross, Joan /kros/
(born 1900) English soprano

crotchet /'krochit/ *n*
a note with the time value of half a minim or 2 quavers – see
illustration at NOTE

crotchet rest *n*
a rest of the same time value as a crotchet

crown /krown/ *n*
1 a crownlike mechanism at the base of a kettledrum that,
controlled by a foot pedal, alters the tension of the head to
tune the drum
2 a piece of wood that passes through the centre of a
handbell and serves to attach the leather handle to the
handguard

crumhorn, krummhorn /'krum,hawn/ *n*
a Renaissance woodwind instrument with a double reed and
a hooked tube

crwth /kroohth/ *n*
an ancient Celtic stringed instrument played by plucking or
with a short bow

Cunningham, Merce /'kuning,h(ə)m/
(born 1919) American choreographer

cup mouthpiece *n*
a mouthpiece (e g of a trumpet or trombone) that is

cup-shaped. In cup-mouthpiece instruments air is made to vibrate by the action of a player's lips.

Curwen, John /'kuhwin/

(1816–80) English music teacher; exponent of the tonic sol-fa method of teaching

Curzon, Sir Clifford Michael /'kuhzən/

(1907–82) English pianist

cut in *vb*

to take 1 of a dancing couple as one's partner

cycle /'siekl/ *n*

a group of works, esp songs, usu on a central theme

cylinder /'silində/ *n*

a mechanism in a music box, that consists of a cylindrical body covered with pins that pluck the required melody tongues when rotated

cymbal /'simbl/ *n*

a concave brass plate that produces a clashing tone when struck with a drumstick or against another cymbal – **cymbalist** *n*

czardas /'chahdash/ *n, pl* **czardas** /~/

a Hungarian dance in which the dancers start slowly and finish rapidly

Czerny, Carl /'chuhni/

(1791–1857) Austrian composer and piano teacher

D

d /dee/ *n, pl* **d's, ds** *often cap*

the 2nd note of a C-major scale

da capo¹ /ˌdah ˈkahpoh/ *adv or adj*

from the beginning

da capo² *n, pl* **da capos**

a passage (to be) repeated da capo

dal segno /ˌdal ˈsaynyoh/ *adv or adj*

from the sign – used to direct the performer to return to the sign that marks the beginning of a repeat

damper /ˈdampə/ *n*

a small felted block which prevents or stops the vibration of a piano string

damper pedal *n*

the pedal that controls the set of dampers on a piano – called also SOFT PEDAL

dance¹ /dahns/ *vb*

to engage in or perform a dance – **danceable** *adj*, **dancer** *n*

dance² *n*

1 (an act or instance or the art of) a series of rhythmic and patterned bodily movements usu performed to music

2 a social gathering for dancing

3 a piece of music for dancing to

dance of death *n*

danse macabre

Dankworth, John /ˈdangkˌwuhth/

(born 1927) English composer and saxophonist

danse macabre /ˌdonhs məˈkahbrə, məˈkahb/ *n*

(a dance symbolizing) a medieval artistic theme in which Death leads people to the grave

danseur /donhˈsuh/ *n*

a male ballet dancer

danseuse /donh'suhz/ *n*
a female ballet dancer

Dart, Robert Thurston /daht/
(1921–71) English conductor, harpsichordist, organist and musicologist

Davie, Alan /'dayvi/
(born 1920) Scottish artist and jazz musician

Davies, Peter Maxwell /'dayviz/
(born 1934) English composer

Davies, Sir Henry Walford
(1869–1941) English organist and composer

Davis, Sir Colin Rex /'dayvis/
(born 1927) English conductor

Davis, Sammy, Jnr
(born 1925) American singer, actor, and dancer

Day, Doris /day/
(born 1924) American actress and singer

D.C. *adv or adj*
da capo

Debussy, Claude Achille /ˌdebooh'si, ˌday-, -'byooh-/
(1862–1918) French composer; works include chamber and orchestral music (e g *L'Après Midi d'un Faune* and *La Mer*), opera and choral music, numerous songs, and piano music

deciso /day'cheezoh/ *adv or adj*
in a decisive manner

decresc. *adv or adj*
decrescendo

decrescendo /ˌdeekrə'shendoh/ *n, adv, or adj, pl*
decrescendos
(a) diminuendo

deep /deep/ *adj*
having a low musical pitch or pitch range – **deeply** *adv*, **deepness** *n*

degree /di'gree/ *n*
1 a line or space of the staff
2 a step, note, or tone of a scale

Delibes, Léo /də'leeb/
(1836–91) French composer, esp of ballets (e g *Coppélia*) and opera

delicato /ˌdeli'kahtoh/ *adv or adj*
in a delicate manner

Delius, Frederick /'dee,liəs/
(1862–1934) English composer of orchestral, choral, and chamber music and opera

Deller, Alfred George /'delə/
(1912–79) English countertenor

de los Angeles, Victoria
– see ANGELES

demisemiquaver /ˌdemisemi'kwayvə/ *n*
a note with the time value of half a semiquaver – see illustration at NOTE

demisemiquaver rest *n*
a rest of the same time value as a demisemiquaver

Denner, Johann Christoph /'denə/
(1655–1707) German maker of recorders, oboes, flutes, and bassoons and developer of the first clarinet

Dent, Edward Joseph /dent/
(1876–1957) English composer, writer, and translator of operas

descant¹ /'des,kant/ *n*
1 the art of composing or improvising contrapuntal part music; *also* the music so composed or improvised
2 treble, soprano
3 a counterpoint superimposed on a simple melody and usu sung by some or all of the sopranos

descant² /des'kant, dis-/ *vi*
to sing or play a descant

descant recorder *n*,
chiefly *Br* the member of the recorder family with the
second highest range

desk /desk/ *n*
a music stand

détaché /ˌday.taˈshay, -ˈ-ˌ-/ *adv or adj*
with breaks between successive tones; with a bow stroke for
each tone – used as a direction to players of bowed
instruments

de Valois, Dame Ninette /də ˈvalwah/
née *Edris Stannus* (born 1898) Irish ballet dancer and
choreographer

develop /diˈveləp/ *vt*
to elaborate by the unfolding of a musical idea and by the
working out of rhythmic and harmonic changes in the theme
– **developable** *adj*

development /diˈveləpmənt/ *n*
the second of usu 3 parts of a movement written in sonata
form, in which the main theme is divided up and elaborated
upon – compare EXPOSITION, RECAPITULATION –
developmental *adj*, **developmentally** *adv*

diapason /ˌdie·əˈpayz(ə)n, -s(ə)n/ *n*
a principal organ stop extending through the range of the
instrument

diatonic /ˌdie·əˈtonik/ *adj*
relating to a major or minor scale of 8 notes to the octave
without chromatic deviation – **diatonically** *adv*

diction /ˈdiksh(ə)n/ *n*
pronunciation and enunciation of words in speaking or
singing – **dictional** *adj*, **dictionally** *adv*

didgeridoo /ˌdijəriˈdooh/ *n*
an Australian wind instrument with a long wooden tube

dim., dimin. *adv or adj*
diminuendo

diminished /di'minisht/ *adj*
of an interval made a semitone less than perfect or minor
<*a ~ fifth*> – compare AUGMENTED, MAJOR, MINOR,
PERFECT

diminuendo /di,minyoo'endoh/ *n, adv, or adj, pl*
diminuendos
(a passage played) with a decrease in volume – see
illustration at DIRECTION

diminution /,dimi'nyoohsh(ə)n/ *n*
the writing of a theme in shorter note values than the
original

direct /di'rekt, die-/ *vt*
to train and usu lead performances of; *specif, chiefly NAm*
to conduct <~ed *the orchestra in a new work*>

direction /di'reksh(ə)n, die-/ *n*
1 the act, art, or technique of directing an orchestra, film,
or theatrical production
2 a word, phrase, or sign indicating the appropriate tempo,
mood, or intensity of a passage or movement – see
illustration

director /di'rektə, die-/ *n*
NAm a conductor

dirge /duhj/ *n*
1 a song or hymn of grief or lamentation, esp intended to
accompany funeral or memorial rites
2 a slow mournful piece of music

disc jockey /'disk ,joki/ *n*
one who introduces records of popular usu contemporary
music (e g at a disco)

disco /'diskoh/ *n, pl* **discos**
1 a dance held mainly for young people to dance to suitable
recorded music, usu introduced by a disc jockey and
accompanied by special lighting effects; *also* the place,
typically a nightclub, where such a dance is held

Directions, Signs, and Symbols

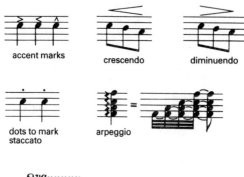

accent marks

crescendo

diminuendo

dots to mark staccato

arpeggio

ottava

pause repeat

alla breve coda segno

tie *or* bind

Ornaments and Decorations

trill *or* shake

mordent

turn

Grace notes

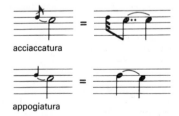

acciaccatura

appoggiatura

2 modern popular music that has a regular beat and is suitable for dancing to in a disco

3 modern dancing that is more or less free-form in style and is performed in time to music having a pronounced beat

4 the equipment and operator necessary for staging a disco <*hiring a ~ for their party*>

discord /'diskawd/ *n*

dissonance

discotheque /'diskə,tek/ *n*

(a) disco

disjunct /dis'jungkt/ *adj*

relating to a melodic progression by intervals larger than a major second

disk, disc /disk/ *n*

1 a mechanism in a music box that consists of a thin flat circular body covered with pins that pluck the required melody tongues when rotated

2 any of the mechanisms that change the pitch of the strings of a harp

dissonance /'disənəns/ *n*

1 a combination of discordant sounds

2 (the sound produced by playing) an unresolved note or chord; *specif* an interval not included in a major or minor triad or its inversions

dissonant /'disənənt/ *adj*

marked by dissonance – **dissonantly** *adv*

Dittersdorf, Carl Ditters von /'dite(ə)s,dawf/

(1739–99) Austrian composer and violinist

ditty /'diti/ *n*

a short simple song

div. *adj*

divisi

diva /'deevə/ *n, pl* **divas, dive** /-vi/

a prima donna

divertimento /di,vuhti'mentoh/ *n, pl* **divertimenti** /-ti/,
   divertimentos
   an instrumental chamber work in several movements and
   usu light in character

divertissement /di'vuhtismənt/ *n, pl* **divertissements**
   /-mənt(s)/
   1 a ballet suite serving as an interlude
   2 a divertimento

Divine Office *n*
   the prescribed forms of prayer and ritual for daily worship
   comprising *Matins, Lauds, Prime, Terce, Sext, None,*
   Vespers, and *Compline* in the Roman Catholic Church and
   Matins and *Evensong* in the Anglican Church

divisi /di'vizee/ *adj*
   separate – used to direct orchestral players reading the same
   staff to divide into 2 or more parts

Dixieland /'diksi,land/ *n*
   jazz music in duple time characterized by collective
   improvisation

dodecaphonic /,doh,dekə'fonik/ *adj*
   twelve-note – **dodecaphonically** *adv*, **dodecaphonist** *n*,
   dodecaphony *n*

doh, do /doh/ *n*
   the first note of the diatonic scale in solmization

dolce /'dohl,chay/ *adv or adj*
   in a soft, sweet, and tender manner

dolcissimo /dohl'chisi,moh/ *adv or adj*
   in a very soft, sweet, and tender manner

dolente /doh'lentay/ *adv or adj*
   in a sorrowful manner

Dolin, Sir Anton /'dohleen/
   né *Patrick Healey-Kay* (born 1904) English ballet dancer
   and choreographer

Dolmetsch, Arnold /'dolmech/

(1858–1940) British (French-born) instrument maker who revived interest in the playing and making of early instruments, particularly the recorder, lute, and keyboard instruments

dolore /doh'lawray/ *n*
grief, sorrow

dominant /'dominənt/ *n*
the fifth note of a diatonic scale – called also FIFTH

Domingo, Placido /do'ming,goh/
(born 1941) Spanish tenor

Donizetti, Gaetano /,doni(t)'zeti/
(1797–1848) Italian composer of operas

doppio /'do(h)pi,oh/ *adj or adv*
double, twice

doppio movimento /,mohvi'mentoh/ *adv or adj*
twice as fast as the preceding

Dorati, Antal /də'rahti/
(born 1906) American (Hungarian-born) conductor

dorian mode /'dawri·ən/ *n, often cap D*
an authentic mode which may be represented on the white keys of the piano on a scale from D to D

dot /dot/ *n*
1 a point after a note or rest indicating augmentation of the time value by one half – see illustration at NOTE
2 a point over or under a note indicating that it is to be played staccato – see illustration at DIRECTION

double bar /,dubl/ *n*
two adjacent vertical lines or a heavy single line marking the end of a principal section of a composition – see illustration at MUSIC

double bass *n*
the largest instrument in the violin family tuned a fifth below the cello – **double bassist** *n*

double bassoon *n*

a contrabassoon

double counterpoint *n*
    2-part counterpoint so constructed that either part may be
    played above or below the other

double dot *n*
    2 points after a note or rest indicating augmentation of the
    time value by three-quarters – see illustration at NOTE

double flat *n*
    a character on the staff indicating a drop in pitch of 2
    semitones – see illustration at MUSIC

double fugue *n*
    a fugue with two subjects

double reed *n*
    two cane reeds bound and vibrating against each other and
    used as the mouthpiece of woodwind instruments of the
    oboe family

double sharp *n*
    a character on the staff indicating a rise in pitch of 2
    semitones – see illustration at MUSIC

double stopping *n*
    the simultaneous playing of 2 strings of a stringed
    instrument

double-tongue *vi*
    to use tongue movements to produce a fast succession of
    detached notes on a wind instrument

Dowland, John /'dowlənd/
    (1563–1626) English composer and lutenist

downbeat /'down,beet/ *n*
    the principally accented (e g the first) note of a bar of music

down-bow /boh/ *n*
    a stroke in playing a bowed instrument (e g a violin) in
    which the bow is drawn across the strings from the heel to
    the tip

doxology /dok'soləji/ *n*

a usu liturgical expression of praise to God

drabant /'dra͵bənt/ *n*
a Polish dance popular in the 18th and early 19th c that included a march and an obertass

draw-stop *n*
a stop

drone /'drohn/ *n*
1 any of the usu 3 pipes on a bagpipe that sound fixed continuous notes
2 an unvarying sustained bass note

drum /drum/ *n*
a percussion instrument usu consisting of a hollow cylinder with a drumhead stretched over each end, that is beaten with a stick or a pair of sticks in playing – **drumlike** *adj*

drumbeat /-͵beet/ *n*
a stroke on a drum or its sound

drumhead /-͵hed/ *n*
the material stretched over the end of a drum

drummer /'drumə/ *n*
one who plays a drum

drumstick /-͵stik/ *n*
a stick for beating a drum

D.S. *adv or adj*
dal segno

Dubois, Théodore /d(y)ooh'bwah/
(1837–1924) French organist and composer

Dufay, Guillaume /dooh'fay/
(*c*1400–1474) French composer

duet /dyooh'et/ *n*
a composition for 2 performers

Dukas, Paul /d(y)ooh'ka/
(1865–1935) French composer; works include the symphonic scherzo *The Sorcerer's Apprentice*

dulciana /͵dulsi'ahnə, -'anə/ *n*

a soft pipe-organ stop having metal pipes and a tone of a soft sweet string quality of 8-foot pitch in the manual organ but 16-foot in the pedal organ

dulcimer /'dulsimə/ *n*
a stringed instrument having strings of graduated length stretched over a sounding board and played with light hammers

dump /dump/ *n*
1 a slow mournful melody or song
2 a dance to such music

Duncan, Isadora /'dungkən/
(1878–1927) American dancer

Dunham, Katherine /'dunəm/
(born 1914) American dancer and choreographer

Dunstable, John /'dunstəbl/
(c1390–1453) English composer

duple /'dyoohpl/ *adj*
marked by 2 or a multiple of 2 beats per bar

duplet /'dyoohplit/ *n*
2 notes performed in the time of 3 of the same value

Du Pré, Jacqueline /ˌd(y)ooh'pray/
'*Mrs Daniel Barenboim*' (born 1945) English cellist

dur /'dooh(ə)/ *adj*
major <*C* ~>

Dvořák, Antonín /də'vaw,zhak/
(1841–1904) Czech composer; works include 9 symphonies, several operas, and choral and chamber music

Dylan, Bob /'dilən/
pseudonym of *Robert Zimmerman* (born 1941) American singer and composer

dynamics /die'namiks/ *n taking sing or pl vb*
variation and contrast in loudness

E

e /ee/ *n, pl* **e's, es** *often cap*
the 3rd note of a C-major scale ·

ear /iə/ *n*
1 the sense or act of hearing
2 sensitivity to musical tone and pitch – **by ear** from
memory of the sound without having seen the written music

echo /'ekoh/ *n, pl* **echoes**
a soft repetition of a phrase – **echoey** *adj*

echo organ *n*
a division of a pipe organ situated at a distance from the rest
of the instrument and containing soft stops suitable for echo
effects

écossaise /,ayko'sez, ,eko-/ *n*
(the music for) a lively folk dance in duple time

Eddy, Nelson /'edi/
(1901–67) American film actor and singer

eight-foot stop , 8-foot stop *n*
a pipe-organ stop sounding the pitches indicated by the
notes, the lowest pipe of such a stop being approximately 8
feet in length – compare FOUR-FOOT STOP, SIXTEEN-FOOT
STOP

eighth /ayt·th/ *n*
an octave

eighth note *n*
NAm a quaver

eighth rest *n*
NAm a rest of the same time value as an eighth note

eightsome reel /'ayts(ə)m/ *n*
a Scottish reel for 8 dancers

ein wenig /,ien 'vaynikh/ *n*
a little – usu in combination

Ek, Gunnar /ek/
(born 1900) Swedish composer

electric /i'lektrik/ *adj,*
of an instrument electronically producing or amplifying
sound <*an ~ organ*>

electronic /i,lek'tronik, ,eelek-/ *adj*
1 electric
2 a term for compositions that include tape-recorded or
synthesized sound

electronic music *n*
music produced by electronic devices

elegy /'eləji/ *n*
a song, poem, or other work expressing sorrow or
lamentation, esp for one who is dead – **elegize** *vb*, **elegiac**
adj, **elegiacal** *adj*, **elegiacally** *adv*

elevation /,eli'vaysh(ə)n/ *n*
(the ability to achieve) a ballet dancer's leap and seeming
suspension in the air – **elevational** *adj*

Elgar, Sir Edward William /'el,gah/
(1857–1934) English composer; works include orchestral
music (e g *Enigma Variations*), oratorios (e g *The Dream of
Gerontius* and *The Kingdom*), other choral music, organ
pieces, and songs

Ellington, Edward Kennedy /'elingtən/
'*Duke Ellington*' (1899–1974) American band leader and
composer

embouchure /,ombooh'shooə/ *n*
the position and use of the lips in playing a wind instrument

enchaînement /on'shenmonh, --'-/ *n*
a short series of steps in ballet (e g linking 2 held poses)
which can be repeated or varied

en dehors /,onh də'haw/ *adv or adj*
1 prominently, emphasized
2 outwards – used of a circular ballet movement of arms or

legs leading away from the body or of the position in which the toes are turned out

energico /enuh'jikoh/ *adv or adj*
with energy

Enesco, Georges /ə'neskoh/
né *George Enescu* (1881–1955) Rumanian violinist and composer

English horn *n*
chiefly NAm a cor anglais

enharmonic /ˌenhah'monik/ *adj*
of or being notes that are written differently (e g A flat and G sharp) but sound the same in the tempered scale – **enharmonically** *adv*

en l'air /ˌon 'leə/ *adv or adj*
of a movement in ballet in the air – compare PAR TERRE

en pressant /ˌonh 'presohn/ *adv or adj*
hurrying

en retenant /ˌenhah 'rətənonh/ *adv or adj*
gradually slower

ensemble /on'sombl/ *n*
1 concerted music of 2 or more parts
2 *taking sing or pl vb*
2a the musicians engaged in the performance of a musical ensemble
2b a group of supporting players, singers, or dancers
3 the quality of togetherness in performance

entr'acte /'ontrakt, -'-/ *n*
(a performance or interlude in) the interval between the acts of a play

entrechat /'ontrəshah/ *n*
a vertical jump into the air during which a ballet dancer repeatedly crosses his/her legs

entrée /'ontray/ *n*
1 a short composition in slow march rhythm, usu in 2

repeated parts, often accompanying the entry of a
procession in an opera or a ballet

2 the opening movement of an opera or ballet following the
overture

3 an introductory movement of any kind

4 any of the ballet numbers in a divertissement

episode /'episohd/ *n*

a digressive subdivision in a composition that is either
derived from the chief thematic material (e g in a fugue) or
is completely new material (e g in a rondo)

epithalamium /,epithə'laymi·əm, -myəm/ *n, pl*
epithalamiums, epithalamia /-mi·ə, -myə/

a song or poem in celebration of a bride and bridegroom

equal temperament *n*

the division of the octave into 12 equal semitones

equal voices *n pl*

voices of the same kind and range

Erard, Sébastien /'erahd/

(1752–1831) French piano maker

espr. *adv or adj*

espressivo

espress. *adv or adj*

espressivo

espressivo /e,spre'sivoh/ *adv or adj*

with expression

ethnomusicology /,ethnoh,myoohzi'koləji/ *n*

the study of the music and instruments, in different cultures,
outside the art music tradition, eg folk music, tribal music –
ethnomusicologist *n*, **ethnomusicological** *adj*

étude /ay'tyoohd/ *n*

a piece of music written primarily for the practice of a
technique; a study

etwas /et'vas/ *adv*

somewhat

euphonium /yooh'fohnyəm, -ni·əm/ *n*
a brass instrument smaller than but resembling a tuba and
having a range from B flat below the bass staff upwards for
3 octaves

eurhythmic , eurythmic /yoo(ə)'ridhmik/ *adj*
of eurhythmics

eurhythmics , eurythmics *n taking sing or pl vb*
the art of bodily movement, esp through expressive timed
movements in response to music

Evans, Sir Geraint Llewellyn /'evənz/
(born 1922) Welsh baritone

execute /'eksi,kyooht/ *vt*
to play, perform <~ *a piece of music*> – **executable** *adj*

execution /,eksi'kyoohsh(ə)n/ *n*
the act, mode, or result of performance <*the* ~ *was perfect
but the piece lacked expression*>

exposition /,ekspə'zish(ə)n/ *n*
1 the first of usu 3 parts of a composition written in sonata
form in which the theme is presented typically in at least 2
contrasting keys – compare DEVELOPMENT,
RECAPITULATION
2 the opening section of a fugue in which the main theme is
stated typically in each of the vocal parts – **expositional** *adj*,
expositor *n*, **expository** *adj*

extempor·ize , -ise /ik'stempə,riez/ *vb*
to compose or perform (something) on the spur of the
moment or impromptu; improvise – **extemporizer** *n*,
extemporization *n*

extravaganza /ik,stravə'ganzə/ *n*
a musical work marked by extreme freedom of style and
structure

F

f /ef/ *n, pl* **f's, fs** *often cap*

the 4th note of a C-major scale

f adv or adj

forte

facile /'fahchilay/ *adv or adj*

easy, easily

fah, fa /fah/ *n*

the 4th note of the diatonic scale in solmization

Falla, Manuel de /'fah,yə, 'fie-/

(1876–1946) Spanish composer, esp of ballets and opera

false /fawls/ *adj*

inaccurate in pitch – **falsely** *adv*, **falseness** *n*, **falsity** *n*

falsetto /fawl'setoh/ *n, pl* **falsettos**

(a singer who uses) an artificially high voice, specif an
artificially produced male singing voice that extends above
the range of the singer's full voice – **falsetto** *adv*, **falsettist** *n*

fancy /'fansi/ *n*

a term for fantasia used by English composers during the
16th and 17th c

fandango /fan'dang·goh/ *n, pl* **fandangos**

(music for) a lively Spanish or Spanish-American dance, usu
performed by a couple to the accompaniment of guitar and
castanets

fanfare /'fan,feə/ *n*

a flourish of trumpets

fantasia /fan'tayzyə, -zh(y)ə/ *n*

1 a free instrumental composition not in strict form

2 a piece comprising familiar tunes

fantasy /'fantəsi/ *n*

a fantasia

farandole /,farən'dohl/ *n*

(music for) a lively Provençal dance in which dancers hold
hands and follow a leader

Fauré, Gabriel Urbain /'foh,ray/
(1845–1924) French composer and organist; works include
songs, chamber and orchestral music, opera, and a Requiem

F clef /ef/ *n*
the bass clef – see illustration at MUSIC

feminine /'femənin/ *adj*
having the final chord occurring on a weak beat – **femininely**
adv

Fenby, Eric William /'fenbi/
(born 1906) English composer and writer, amanuensis to
Delius during the latter's final years

fermata /fuh'mahtə/ *n*
a prolongation at the discretion of the performer of a note,
chord, or rest; *also* a pause

Ferrier, Kathleen /'feri·ə/
(1912–53) English contralto

feurig /'foyrikh/ *adv or adj*
in a fiery manner

ff , *fff adv or adj*
fortissimo

fiddle[1] /'fidl/ *n*
a violin

fiddle[2] *vi*
to play on a fiddle – **fiddler** *n*

Fiedler, Arthur /'feedlə/
(1894–1979) American conductor

Field, John /feeld/
(1782–1837) Irish composer and pianist who invented the
name and style of the nocturne

Fields, Dame Gracie /fee(ə)ldz/
née *Stansfield* (1898–1979) English singer and comedienne

fife /fief/ *n*

a small flute used chiefly to accompany the drum

fifteenth /fif'teenth/ *n*
1 a 2-foot stop in a pipe organ
2 an interval or compass of a double octave

fifth /fith; *also* filth/ *n*
1 (the harmonic combination of 2 notes at) an interval of 5 diatonic degrees
2 a note at this interval; *specif* the dominant – **fifth** *adj*

figurant /'fig(y)ərənt/ , *fem* **figurante** /-'ront/ *n*
a ballet dancer who dances only in a group

figuration /ˌfigyoo'raysh(ə)n/ *n*
ornamentation of a passage by using musical figures

figure¹ /'figə/ *n*
1 a series of movements in a dance
2 a short phrase

figure² *vt*
1 to embellish with passing notes or figures
2 to write figures over or under (the bass) in order to indicate the accompanying chords – **figurer** *n*

figured bass *n*
a way of notating a continuo

filar la voce /ˌfeelah ˌla 'vohchay/ *n, adj, or adv*
– used as a direction in singing to indicate the sustaining of a note for a long time with one breath, usu with a crescendo and a diminuendo

finale /fi'nahli/ *n*
1 the last section of an instrumental composition
2 a final scene or number in (an act of) a public performance

fine /'fi,nay/ *n*
the end – used to mark the closing point after a repeat

finger /'fing·gə/ *vt*
1 to play (an instrument) with the fingers
2 to play (e g notes or chords) with a specific fingering

3 to mark fingerings on (a score) as a guide in playing

fingerboard /-,bawd/ *n*
the part of a stringed instrument against which the fingers press the strings to vary the pitch

finger hole *n*
any of the openings in the tube of a wind instrument that, when covered by the fingers, affect its length and hence alter the pitch

fingering /'fing·gəring/ *n*
(the marking indicating) the use or position of the fingers in sounding notes on an instrument

Finzi, Gerald /'finzi/
(1901–56) English composer esp of vocal works

fioritura /fee,awri'toora/ *n*
decoration of a melody, esp by vocalists and violinists, that was usu improvised and was popular esp in the 18th c

fipple /'fipl/ *n*
a grooved plug in the end of a whistle, flute, or organ pipe

fipple flute *n*
a tubular wind instrument characterized mainly by a whistle mouthpiece and finger holes

first /fuhst/ *adj or n*
(relating to or having) the (most prominent and) usu highest part among a group of instruments or voices

first movement form *n*
sonata form

Fischer-Dieskau, Dietrich /,fishə 'deeskow/
(born 1925) German baritone

Fitzgerald, Ella /,fits'jerəld/
(born 1918) American singer

flageolet /,flajə'let/ *n*
a small fipple flute

Flagstad, Kirsten /'flag,stat/
(1895–1962) Norwegian soprano

flam /flam/ *n*
a drumbeat of 2 strokes, the first being a very quick grace note

flamenco /flə'mengkoh/ *n, pl* **flamencos**
(music suitable for) a vigorous rhythmic dance (style) of the Andalusian gypsies

flat¹ /flat/ *adj*
1 *of a note* lowered a semitone in pitch
2 lower than the proper pitch – **flatly** *adv*, **flatness** *n*, **flattish** *adj*

flat² *n*
(a character indicating) a note 1 semitone lower than a specified or particular note – see illustration at MUSIC

flat³ *adv*
below the proper pitch

flatten /'flat(ə)n/ *vt*
to lower in pitch, esp by a semitone – **flattener** *n*

flautist /'flawtist/ *n*
one who plays a flute

fleshings /'fleshingz/ *n pl*
flesh-coloured tights worn by dancers and actors

flicorno /fli'kawnoh/ *n, pl* **flicorni** /-ni/
a brass instrument resembling a bugle; *broadly* the Italian equivalent to the saxhorn and flügelhorn

fling /'fling/ *n*
a Scottish dance, resembling a vigorous reel, popular in the Highlands

flourish /'flurish/ *n*
a showy or flowery embellishment or passage

flue pipe /'flooh/ *n*
an organ pipe whose tone is produced by an air current striking the lip and causing the air within to vibrate – compare REED PIPE

flügelhorn, flugelhorn /'floohgl,hawn/ *n*

a valved brass instrument resembling a cornet; *broadly* the German equivalent of the saxhorn

flute /flooht/ *n*

1 a keyed woodwind instrument that consists of a cylindrical tube stopped at one end, is played by blowing air across a side hole, and has a range from middle C upwards for 3 octaves

2 **flute, flute stop** a flue pipe-organ stop of flute quality and of 8-foot or 4-foot pitch – **flutelike** *adj*

flutist /'floohtist/ *n*,
chiefly NAm a flautist

Fokine, Michel /'fohkeen, -'-/
(1880–1942) American (Russian-born) choreographer

folía /foh'leeə/ *n*
a noisy carnival dance of Portuguese origin

folk music, folk /fohk/ *n*
simple music, usu song, of traditional origin or style

folksinger /'fohksingə/ *n*
one who sings folk songs – **folksinging** *n*

folk song *n*
(a contemporary song in the style of) a simple song of traditional origin that is characterized by stanzaic form, refrain, and repeating melody

Fonteyn, Dame Margot /fon'tayn, '-,-/
née *Margot Hookham* (born 1919) English dancer

foot /foot/ *n*
the terminal section of a wind instrument; *specif* the lowest part of an organ pipe

forlana /faw'lahnə/ , **furlana** /fuhr-/ *n, pl* **forlane** /-nay/, **forlanas**
(the music for) a lively old Italian dance in ⅜ or ⁶⁄₄ time

forte /'fawti, -tay/ *n, adv, or adj*
(a note or passage played) loudly

fortepiano /,fawtipi'anoh/ *n*

a piano of the late 18th century

forte-piano /ˌfawti'pyahnoh/ *adv or adj*
loud then immediately soft

fortissimo /faw'tisimoh/ *adv or adj*
very loud

forza /'fawtsə/ *n*
force

forzando /ˌfaw'tsandoh/ *adj or adv*
forcing; with a sudden accent

Foster, Stephen Collins /'fostə/
(1826–64) American composer

fouetté /fooh'etay/ *n*
a quick whipping movement of the raised leg in ballet dancing

foundation stop *n*
1 a stop in a pipe organ whose pipes are in unison with one or more octaves higher or lower than the piano strings sounded by the corresponding keys – compare MUTATION STOP
2 any of the fundamental flue stops (e g the diapasons) as contrasted with reed stops or mixture stops

four-foot stop, 4-foot stop *n*
a pipe-organ stop sounding pitches an octave higher than the notes indicate – compare EIGHT-FOOT STOP

four-handed /ˌfaw-/ *adj*
of keyboard music for 4 hands, i.e. for piano duet

Fournier, Pierre /'fawni·ay/
(born 1906) French cellist

fourth /fawth/ *n*
1 (the harmonic combination of 2 notes at) an interval of 4 diatonic degrees
2 a note at this interval; *specif* the subdominant – **fourth** *adj*

fox-trot /'foks,trot/ *vi or n*
(to dance) a ballroom dance that includes slow walking and

quick running steps

fp *adv or adj*
forte-piano (loud quiet)

Franck, César Auguste /frangk/
(1822–90) Belgian composer and organist; works include orchestral and chamber music, choral, church, and secular pieces, and opera

Frankel, Benjamin /'frankl/
(1906–73) English composer

free fantasia *n*
a term for the development section in a sonata-form movement

French horn *n*
1 a circular valved brass instrument with a usual range from B below the bass staff upwards for more than 3 octaves
2 an 8-foot pipe-organ reed stop having a quality similar to that of a French horn

Frescobaldi, Girolamo /ˌfreskəˈboldi/
(1583–1643) Italian organist and composer, esp of keyboard works

fret /fret/ *n*
a ridge fixed across the fingerboard of a stringed instrument (e g a guitar)

Friml, Charles Rudolf /'friml/
(1879–1972) American (Czech-born) composer

fuga /'fyoohgə/ *n*
a fugue

fugal /'fyoohgl/ *adj*
in the style of a fugue – **fugally** *adv*

fugato /fooh'gahtoh/ *n, adv, or adj, pl* **fugatos**
(a musical passage) in the style but not in the strict form of a fugue

fughetta /f(y)ooh'getə/ *n*
a short fugue

fugue /fyoohg/ *n*

a composition in which 1 or 2 themes, or subjects, are repeated or imitated by successively entering voices or instruments and are contrapuntally developed in a continuous interweaving of the parts – **fuguist** *n*

full close *n*

a perfect cadence

full score *n*

a score comprising all the parts of a composition, vocal and orchestral, placed one above the other in the order: woodwind, brass, percussion, harp and keyboard instruments, solo instrument(s), voices, 1st and 2nd violins, violas, cellos, and double basses

fundamental¹ /ˌfundəˈmentl/ *adj*

1 *of a chord or its position* having the root in the bass

2 of or produced by a fundamental – **fundamentally** *adv*

fundamental² *n*

1 the prime note of a harmonic series

2 the root of a chord

funk /fungk/ *n*

funky music

funky /ˈfungki/ *adj*

having an earthy unsophisticated style and feeling (e g as in the blues) – **funkiness** *n*

fuoco /fyoohˈohkoh/ *n*

fire; *con fuoco* with fire

furiant /ˈf(y)ooəriˌont, ˌ--ˈ-/ *n*

a spirited Bohemian dance tune with shifting accents

furioso /ˌfyooəriˈohsoh/ *adv or adj*

with great force or vigour

Furtwängler, Wilhelm /ˈfooətˌvenglə/

(1886–1954) German conductor

futurism /ˈfyoohchəˌriz(ə)m/ *n*

a movement in art, music, and literature begun in Italy

about 1910 and seeking to express the dynamic energy and
movement of mechanical processes – **futurist** *n or adj*
futuristic /ˌfyoohchə'ristik/ *adj*
of the future or futurism; *esp* bearing no relation to known
or traditional forms; ultramodern – **futuristically** *adv*
fz adj or adv
rare equivalent of *sf* – sforzando

G

g /jee/ *n, pl* **g's, gs** *often cap*
the 5th note of a C-major scale

Gabrieli, Andrea /ˌgabri'eli/
(*c*1510–86) Italian composer and organist

Gabrieli, Giovanni
nephew of Andrea, (*c*1555–1612) Italian organist and composer, esp of choral and ensemble music

galliard /'galyəd/ *n*
(music in time for) a lively dance in triple time popular in the 16th and 17th c and often paired with a pavane

Galli-Curci, Amelita /ˌgali'kuhchi/
née *Galli* (?1889–1963) American (Italian-born) soprano

galop /'galəp/ *n*
(music for) a lively dance in duple time popular in the 19th c

galopade, gallopade /ˌgalə'pahd/ *n*
a galop

Galway, James /'gawlway/
(born 1939) British flautist

gamba /'gambə/ *n*
1 abbreviation for *viola da gamba*
2 a labial pipe-organ stop of 16-foot pitch and string quality

gamelan /'gami,lan/ *n*
an Indonesian ensemble of wind, string and percussion (including gongs)

gamut /'gamət/ *n*
the whole series of recognized notes

gangar /ˌgan'gah/ *n*
a walking dance from Norway

Garden, Mary /'gahd(ə)n/
(1874–1967) American (Scottish-born) soprano

Garland, Judy /'gahlənd/

née *Frances Gumm* (1922–69) American film actress and singer

gauche /gohsh/ *n or adj*
(the) left

gavotte /gə'vot/ *n*
(a composition or movement in moderately quick ¾ time for) an 18th-c dance in which the feet are raised rather than slid – **gavotte** *vi*

G clef /'jee/ *n*
the treble clef – see illustration at MUSIC

Gedda, Nicolai /'gedə/
(born 1925) Swedish tenor

gedeckt /gə'dekt/ , **gedackt** *also* **gedact** /-dahkt, -dakt/ *n*
a labial pipe-organ stop of 2-foot, 4-foot, 8-foot, 16-foot, or 32-foot pitch and of flute quality

geigen principal, geigen /'giegən/ *n*
a metal labial pipe-organ stop of 8-foot pitch with a combination of diapason and string quality

gemshorn /'gem(p)s,hawn, 'gemz-/ *n*
1 a medieval recorder made from a chamois horn
2 a soft pipe-organ stop

Genée, Dame Adeline /jə'nay/
née *Anita Jensen* (1878–1970) British (Danish-born) ballet dancer

general pause *n*
a rest in all parts in ensemble or orchestral music; abbreviated to GP in scores

German, Edward /'juhmən/
(1862–1936) English composer of incidental music, operettas (e g *Merrie England* and *Tom Jones*), and orchestral works

Gershwin, George /'guhsh,win/
(1898–1937) American jazz pianist and composer; works include *Rhapsody in Blue* and *An American in Paris*

geschwind /ge'shvint/ *adv or adj*
 quick
Gibbons, Orlando /'gibənz/
 (1583–1625) English composer and organist; works include
 madrigals, church music, and music for viols and virginals
Gibson, Sir Alexander Drummond /'gibsən/
 (born 1926) Scottish conductor
Gieseking, Walter Wilhelm /'geezə,king/
 (1895–1956) German (French-born) pianist
gig /gig/ *n*
 a musician's engagement for a specified time; *esp* such an
 engagement for 1 performance
Gigli, Beniamino /'zheeli/
 (1890–1957) Italian tenor
gigue /zheeg/ *n*
 a lively dance in compound triple rhythm and consisting of 2
 sections, each of which is repeated – compare JIG
Gilbert, Sir William Schwenck /'gilbət/
 (1836–1911) English librettist and poet; collaborated with
 Sir Arthur Sullivan in many operettas
Gillespie, John Birks /gi'les,pi/
 '*Dizzy*' (born 1917) American bandleader and trumpeter
giocoso /joh'kohsoh/ *adv or adj*
 in a playful or humorous manner
giojoso *also* **gioioso** /joh'yohsoh/ *adv or adj*
 in a joyous and gay manner
gittern /'gituhn/ *n*
 a medieval guitar
Giulini, Carlo Maria /jooh'leeni/
 (born 1914) Italian conductor
giusto /'jooh,stoh/ *adj*
 strict, exact <*tempo* ~>
Glazunov, Alexander /'glazə,nov, -,nof, ,glazoo'-/
 (1865–1936) Russian composer of orchestral and choral

works and chamber music

glee /glee/ *n*

an unaccompanied song for 3 or more, usu male voices

glee club *n*

a chorus, esp in the USA, organized for singing usu short secular pieces

glide /glied/ *n*

a portamento

Glinka, Mikhail Ivanovich /'glingkə/

(1804–57) Russian composer; works include two operas, *A Life for the Tsar* and *Ruslan and Ludmila*

glissade /gli'sahd/ *n*

a gliding step in ballet

glissando /gli'sandoh/ *n, pl* **glissandi** /-di/, **glissandos**

a rapid sliding up or down the scale

glockenspiel /'glokən,speel, -,shpeel/ *n*

a percussion instrument consisting of a series of graduated metal bars played with 2 hammers

Glossop, Peter /'glosəp/

(born 1928) English baritone

Glover, Sarah Anna /'gluvə/

(1786–1867) English music teacher; invented tonic sol-fa system of notation

Gluck, Christoph Willibald /glook/

(1714–87) German composer, esp of operas

Gobbi, Tito /'gobi/

(1915–84) Italian baritone

go-go /'goh ,goh/ *adj*

of or being the music or a style of dance performed or a dancer performing at a disco

gong /gong/ *n*

a circular percussion instrument that produces a resounding tone when struck with a usu padded hammer – **gong** *vi*

Goodman, Benny /'goodmən/

(born 1909) American clarinettist and band leader

Goossens, Eugene /'goohsəns/
(1893–1962) English conductor and composer

Goossens, Leon
brother of Eugene, (born 1897) English oboist

gopak /'goh,pak/ *n*
a Ukrainian folk dance with heel beats

gospel /'gospl/ *adj*
of or being usu evangelistic religious songs of American origin

Gould, Glenn /goohld/
(1932–82) Canadian pianist and composer

Gounod, Charles François /'gooh,noh/
(1818–93) French composer; works include operas (e g *Faust*), oratorios, and church and orchestral music

G.P. *n*
general pause

grace /grays/ *n*
a trill, turn, or appoggiatura

grace note *n*
a note added as an ornament – see illustration at DIRECTION

gradual /'gradyooəl, -jooəl, -jəl/ *n*
a book containing the chants for the Mass

Graham, Martha /'grayəm/
(born 1894?) American dancer

Grainger, Percy Aldridge /'graynjə/
(1882–1961) Australian pianist and composer; took part in revival of English folk music, collecting and arranging many songs

granadina /,granə'deenə/ *n*
a fandango of Granada, Spain, with the same harmonic and vocal peculiarities as the malagueña

grand /grand/ *n*
a grand piano

grande pirouette /grond/ *n*
a pirouette in which the free leg is held out at right angles
while the revolution is made

grandioso /ˌgrandi'ohsoh, -zoh/ *adv or adj*
in a broad and noble style

grand opera *n*
opera with a serious dramatic plot and often no spoken
dialogue

grand piano *n*
a piano with horizontal frame and strings

grave /'grah,vay/ *adv or adj*
in a slow and solemn manner

grazia /'gratsiə/ *n*
grace

grazioso /ˌgratsi'ohsoh, -zoh/ *adv*
gracefully

great organ /grayt/ *n*
the principal division of an organ including the loudest stops

Gregorian chant /gri'gawri·ən/ *n*
a rhythmically free liturgical plainsong, associated with
Pope Gregory I, which became used in the Roman Catholic
church

Gregorian tone *n*
any of 8 plainsong melodies of Gregorian chant prescribed
for the psalms in the Roman Catholic church, in 1 of the 8
modes

Grétry, André Ernest Modeste /'graytri/
(1741–1813) Belgian composer, esp of comic operas

Grey, Beryl /gray/
(born 1927) English ballet dancer

Grieg, Edvard Hagerup /greeg/
(1843–1907) Norwegian composer; works include the
incidental music for *Peer Gynt* and the piano concerto in A
minor

ground bass /bays/ *n*
a short bass passage continually repeated below constantly changing melody and harmony

group /groohp/ *n*
a usu small number of players of popular music, sometimes including a singer

Grove, Sir George /grohv/
(1820–1900) English writer on music; famous for *Grove's Dictionary of Music and Musicians*

Groves, Sir Charles Bernard /grohvz/
(born 1915) English conductor

Grumiaux, Arthur /'groohmi·oh/
(born 1921) Belgian violinist

Guarneri /gwah'ne(ə)ri/
Italian family of violin makers: esp **Giuseppe Antonio** (1687–1745)

Guido d'Arezzo, Guido Aretino /ˌgwidoh dəˈretsoh/, /ˌarəˈtinoh/
(*c*991–after 1033) music theorist who devised system of solmization

guitar /gi'tah/ *n*
a flat-bodied stringed instrument with a long fretted neck, plucked with a plectrum or the fingers – **guitarist** *n*

Guthrie, Woodrow Wilson /'guthri/
'*Woody*' (1912–67) American folksinger

H

habanera /ˌhabəˈnyeərə/ *n*
(music for) a Cuban dance in slow duple time

Haitink, Bernard /ˈhietingk/
(born 1929) Dutch conductor

Haley, Bill /ˈhayli/
(1925–81) American rock and roll singer

half close *n*
an imperfect cadence

half note *n*,
NAm a minim

half rest *n*
NAm a rest of the same time value as a half note

half step *n*
NAm a semitone

halftone /ˈhahftohn/ *n*
a semitone

hallelujah /ˌhaliˈloohyə/ *n or interj*
(an) alleluia

Hallé, Sir Charles /ˈhalay/
(1819–95) English (German-born) conductor

halling /ˈholing, ˈhal-/ *n*
(the music for) an acrobatic Norwegian dance in duple time
for 1 to 3 single dancers

hammer /ˈhamə/ *n*
1 a lever with a striking head for ringing a bell or striking a
gong
2 a padded mallet in a piano action for striking a string
3 a hand mallet for playing various percussion instruments

Hammond, Dame Joan Hood /ˈhamənd/
(born 1912) Australian (New-Zealand-born) soprano

hanacca /ˌhanəˈkə/ *n*

a Moravian dance in triple time resembling a quick
polonaise

handbell /'hand,bel/ *n*

a small bell with a handle; *esp* any of a set of small bells
tuned in a scale

Handel, George Frideric /handl/

(1685–1759) British (German-born) composer; works
include many operas, oratorios (e g *Messiah*), chamber and
church music, songs, and orchestral works

Handy, William Christopher /'handi/

'WC' (1873–1958) American blues musician

hard rock *n*

basic rock music played in its original style

harmonic¹ /hah'monik/ *adj*

of harmony, a harmonic, or harmonics – **harmonically** *adv*,
harmonicalness *n*

harmonic² *n*

1 a note in a harmonic series

2 a flutelike tone produced on a stringed instrument by
touching a vibrating string at a point (e g the midpoint)
which divides it into halves, thirds, etc

harmonica /hah'monikə/ *n*

a small rectangular wind instrument with free reeds recessed
in air slots from which notes are sounded when the player
breathes out and in

harmonics /hah'moniks/ *n taking sing or pl vb*

the study of the physical characteristics of music

harmonic series *n*

a set of tones consisting of a fundamental and all the
overtones whose frequency ratio to it can be expressed in
whole numbers

harmonious /hah'monyəs, -ni·əs/ *adj*

musically concordant – **harmoniously** *adv*, **harmoniousness** *n*

harmonist /'hahmənist/ *n*

one who is skilled in harmony – **harmonistic** *adj*,
harmonistically *adv*

harmonium /hah'mohni·əm, -nyəm/ *n*
a reed organ in which pedals operate a bellows that forces
air through free reeds

harmon·ize, -ise /'hahmənicz/ *vb*
1 *vi* to play or sing in harmony
2 *vt* to provide or accompany with harmony

harmony /'hahməni/ *n*
1 the (pleasant-sounding) combination of simultaneous
notes in a chord
2 the structure of music with respect to the composition and
progression of chords

harp /hahp/ *n*
an instrument that has strings stretched across an open
triangular frame and is played by plucking with the fingers –
harpist *n*

harper /'hahpə/ *n*
a harp player

harpsichord /'hahpsi‚kawd/ *n*
a chromatic keyboard instrument having a horizontal frame
and strings and producing notes by the action of quills or
leather points plucking the strings – **harpsichordist** *n*

Harris, Roy /'haris/
(1898–1979) American composer

Harrison, George /'harisən/
(born 1943) English musician; member of the *Beatles*

Hart, Moss /haht/
(1904–61) American librettist and dramatist

Harty, Sir (Herbert) Hamilton /'hahti/
(1879–1941) Irish conductor and composer

hautboy, hautbois /'ohboy/ *n*
archaic an oboe

haute danse /‚(h)oht 'dahns/ *n*

dancing in which the feet are lifted from the ground

Hawaiian guitar *n*
a steel guitar

hay, hey /hay/ *n*
a rustic dance featuring winding and interweaving dance figures

Haydn, (Franz) Joseph /hiedn/
(1732–1809) Austrian composer; his many works include 104 symphonies, operas, masses, string quartets, and keyboard sonatas

head /hed/ *n*
1 the uppermost section or joint of an instrument (e g a recorder or flute)
2 the end of a drum
3 the point of a violin bow
4 the pegbox and scroll of a bowed instrument
5 the oval part of a printed note

headstock *n*
a pivoted crossbeam that supports a church bell

heavy /'hevi/ *adj*,
of rock music loud and strongly rhythmic – **heaviness** *n*

Heckel /'hekl/
German family of wind instrument makers: father, **Johann Adam** (1812–77), and son, **Wilhelm** (1856–1909), greatly improved instruments such as the bassoon and contrabassoon, and Wilhelm invented the heckelphone

heckelphone /'hekl,fohn/ *n*
a baritone oboe with a pitch intermediate between a cor anglais and a bassoon and having a long tube ending in a spherical bell provided with a foot on which the instrument stands

Heifetz, Jascha /'hiefits/
(born 1901) American (Russian-born) violinist

Heldentenor /'heldn,tenə/ *n*

a tenor with a dramatic voice suited to heroic roles

helicon /'helikən/ *n*
a large circular tuba similar to a sousaphone

hemidemisemiquaver /ˌhemiˌdemiˌsemi'kwayvə/ *n*
a note with the time value of half a demisemiquaver – see illustration at NOTE

hemidemisemiquaver rest *n*
a rest of the same time value as a hemidemisemiquaver

hemiola /ˌhemi'ohlə/ *n*
a rhythmic alteration consisting of 3 beats in place of 2 or 2 beats in place of 3

Henze, Hans Werner /'hentsə/
(born 1926) German composer, esp of operas

Hess, Dame Myra /hes/
(1890–1965) English pianist

hexachord /'heksəˌkawd/ *n*
a diatonic series of six notes having a semitone between the third and fourth notes

hey /hay/ *n*
a hay

Highland fling *n*
a lively solo Scottish folk dance

Hindemith, Paul /'hindəˌmit(h)/
(1895–1963) American (German-born) viola player and composer of chamber, orchestral music and opera

hipster /'hipstə/ *n*
someone who is unusually aware of and interested in new and unconventional patterns, esp in jazz

hitch pin *n*
any of a row of slanting metal pins in a piano action to which the strings are attached at the ends opposite the tuning pins

hit parade *n*
a group or listing of popular songs ranked in order of the

number of records of each sold

hobbyhorse /'hobi,haws/ n

a figure of a horse fastened round the waist of a performer in a morris dance

hoedown /'hoh,down/ n,

chiefly NAm a gathering featuring square dances

Hofmann, Josef /'hofmən/

(1876–1957) Polish pianist

hohlflöte /'hohl,fluhtə/ , **hohl flute** n

a pipe-organ flute stop usu in 8-foot pitch with a dull hollow quality

Holiday, Billie /'holiday/

(1915–59) American jazz singer

Holliger, Heinz /'holigə/

(born 1939) Swiss oboist

Holst, Gustav Theodore /hohlst/

(1874–1934) English composer; works include the orchestral suite *The Planets* and the choral piece *Hymn of Jesus*

Holst, Imogen

daughter of Gustav, (1907–84) English composer, conductor, and writer, esp of books on her father

homophonic /,homə'fonik/ adj

of or being music in which all the parts move together, the opposite of polyphony – compare POLYPHONIC –

homophony n

Honegger, Arthur /,onay'ge(ə), '(h)onigə/

(1892–1955) French (Swiss-born) composer, esp of chamber and orchestral music

honky-tonk /'hongki ,tongk/ n

a form of ragtime piano playing – **honky-tonk** adj

honour, *NAm chiefly* **honor** /'onə/ vt

to salute (e g one's partner) with a bow in a country dance

horn /hawn/ n

1 an animal's horn used as a wind instrument

2 a hunting horn

3 a French horn

4 a wind instrument used in a jazz band; *esp* a trumpet

5 a tenor saxhorn used in a military band – **horn** *adj*, **hornlike** *adj*

hornpipe /-ˌpiep/ *n*

(a piece of music for) a lively British folk dance typically associated with sailors

Horowitz, Vladimir /ˈhorəˌvits/

(born 1904) American (Russian-born) pianist

Horsley, Colin /ˈhawsli/

(born 1920) British pianist

hot /hot/ *adj*

of or being an exciting style of jazz with strong rhythms and free melodic improvisation – compare COOL, STRAIGHT

Hotter, Hans /ˈhotə/

(born 1909) Austrian (German-born) baritone

Hotteterre /ˈhotəˌteə/

French family of wind instrument and hurdy-gurdy makers: *esp* **Jacques** (*c*1684–*c*1761)

Howells, Sir Herbert /ˈhowəlz/

(1892–1983) English composer

hula *also* **hula-hula** /ˈhoolə/ *n*

a Polynesian dance involving swaying of the hips

hum /hum/ *vt*

1 to sing with the lips closed and without articulation

2 to affect or express by humming – **hum** *n*

Hummel, Johann Nepomuk /ˈhooml/

(1778–1837) Austrian pianist and composer, esp of piano works

hum note *n*

a tone produced by a bell, that persists after the strike note and overtones have died out. In an accurately tuned bell the hum note is an octave below the strike note.

humoreske, humoresque /ˌhyoomə'resk/ *n*
a composition that is whimsical or fanciful in character

Humperdinck, Engelbert /'hoompə,dingk, 'hum-/
(1854–1921) German composer; works include the opera
Hansel and Gretel

Hunter, Rita /'huntə/
(born 1933) English soprano

hunting horn *n*
a signal horn used in the chase, usu consisting of a long
coiled tube with a flared bell

hurdy-gurdy /ˌhuhdi 'guhdi/ *n*
an instrument in which the sound is produced by turning a
crank; *esp* a barrel organ

hymn¹ /him/ *n*
a song of praise or joy

hymn² *vb*
1 *vt* to praise or worship in hymns
2 *vi* to sing a hymn

I

ictus /'iktəs/ *n*
rhythmic or metrical stress

idyll, idyl /'idil/ *n*
a pastoral or romantic composition

imitation /ˌimi'taysh(ə)n/ *n*
the repetition in one part of the melodic theme, phrase, or
motive previously found in another part – **imitational** *adj*

immer /'imə/ *adv*
always, constantly

imperfect /im'puhfikt/ *adj,*
of a cadence passing to a dominant chord from a tonic chord

impetuoso /im,petyoo'ohsoh, -zoh/ *adv or adj*
in an impetuous manner

impressionist /im'preshənist/ *adj*
a term borrowed from painting and applied to the music of
e g Debussy and Ravel

impromptu /im'promptyooh/ *n*
a composition usu for piano suggesting improvisation

improvise /'imprəviez/ *vb*
to compose or perform spontaneously without a musical
score – **improviser** *n*, **improvisation** *n*, **improvisatory** *adj*

in alt /ˌeen 'alt/ *adv or adj*
in the octave beginning with the second G above middle C
<ranging up to E ~>

in altissimo /al'tisimoh/ *adv or adj*
in the octave beginning with the third G above middle C

incalzando /ˌeenkal'tsandoh/ *adv or adj*
with increasing speed and usu increasing tone

incidental music /ˌinsi'dentl/ *n*
music composed for a play

Indy, (Paul Marie Théodore) Vincent d' /'dandi/

(1851–1931) French composer; works include operas,
symphonies, tone poems, and chamber music

inflect /in'flekt/ *vb*

to change or vary the pitch of (e g the voice); modulate

inflexion, inflection /in'fleksh(ə)n/ *n*

1 change or variation of pitch or loudness; modulation of
the voice in speaking or singing

2 a modification in pitch or dynamics in a musical line

3 a change from the monotone in liturgical chanting

inharmonious /,inhah'mohnyəs, -ni·əs/ *adj*

not harmonious – **inharmoniously** *adv*

instrument /'instrəmənt/ *n*

a device used to produce music

instrumental[1] /,instrə'mentl/ *adj*

relating to, composed for, or performed on a musical
instrument – **instrumentally** *adv*

instrumental[2] *n*

a composition or passage for instruments but not voice

instrumentalist /,instrə'mentl,ist/ *n*

a player of a musical instrument

instrumentation /,instrəmən'taysh(ə)n, -men-/ *n*

the arrangement or composition of music for instruments

interlude /'intə,loohd/ *n*

a piece of music played between the parts of a longer
composition, a drama, etc or between other whole pieces

intermezzo /,intə'metsoh/ *n, pl* **intermezzi** /-see/,
intermezzos

1 a movement between the major sections of an extended
work (e g an opera)

2 a short independent instrumental composition often for
piano

interrupted /,intə'ruptid/ *adj,*

of a cadence passing from a dominant chord to some chord,
usu the submediant, other than the tonic

interval /'intəv(ə)l/ *n*
the difference in pitch between 2 notes

intonate /'intohnayt/ *vt*
to intone, utter

intonation /,intə'naysh(ə)n/ *n*
1 the act of intoning; *esp* liturgical chanting
2 something that is intoned; *specif* the opening notes of a Gregorian chant
3 performance of music with respect to correctness of pitch and harmony

intone /in'tohn/ *vb*
to utter (something) in musical or prolonged tones; recite in singing tones or in a monotone – **intoner** *n*

introduction /,intrə'duksh(ə)n/ *n*
a short introductory passage

introit /'introyt/ *n*
a piece of music sung or played at the beginning of a church service; *specif, often cap* the antiphon or psalm sung as the priest approaches the altar to celebrate the Eucharist

invention /in'vensh(ə)n/ *n*
a short keyboard composition, usu in double counterpoint

inversion /in'vuhsh(ə)n/ *n*
the process or result of changing, converting, or reversing the relative positions of the elements of an interval, chord, or phrase – **inversive** *adj*

invert /in'vuht/ *vt*
to subject to inversion – **invertible** *adj*

ionian mode /ie'ohni·ən/ *n, often cap I*
an authentic mode which may be represented on the white keys of the piano on a scale from C to C

Ireland, John /'ierlənd/
(1879–1962) English composer

Iturbi, José /i'tuhbi/
(1895–1980) Spanish-born pianist and conductor

Ives, Charles Edward /ievz/
(1874–1954) American composer of symphonies and choral and chamber works; recognized as pioneer of modern American music

J

jack /jak/ *n*

an intermediate upright piece of wood at the inner end of each key in any of several keyboard instruments (e g a piano or harpsichord) communicating its action to the string by means of a guide, a metal tangent, or a hammer

jam /jam/ *vi*

to take part in a jam session

jam session *n*

an impromptu jazz performance that features group improvisation

Janáček, Leoš /'yanə,chek/

(1854–1928) Czech composer; works include the operas *Jenufa* and *The Cunning Little Vixen* and the *Glagolitic Mass*

Janequin, Clément /'yanə,kan/

(*c*1485–1558) French composer

Jaques-Dalcroze, Émile /,zhak,dal'krohz/

(1865–1950) Swiss composer and creator of eurhythmics

jazz /jaz/ *n*

1 music developed esp from ragtime and blues and characterized by syncopated rhythms, contrapuntal ensemble playing, and individual or group improvisation around a basic theme or melody

2 popular dance music influenced by jazz and played in a loud rhythmic manner

jazzer /'jazə/ *n*

a jazzman

jazzman /'jazman, -mən/ *n*

a jazz musician

jazz up *vt*

to play (a piece of music) in the style of jazz

jazzy /'jazi/ *adj*
    having the characteristics of jazz – **jazzily** *adv*, **jazziness** *n*

jeté /zhə'tay/ *n*
    a high arching leap in ballet in which the dancer has one leg
    stretched forwards and the other backwards

Jew's harp, Jews' harp *n*
    a small lyre-shaped instrument that is placed between the
    teeth and sounded by striking a metal tongue with the finger

jig¹ /jig/ *n*
    (a piece of music for) a lively springy dance in triple time –
    compare GIGUE

jig² *vb*
    to dance in the rapid lively manner of a jig

jitterbug /'jitə,bug/ *n*
    (one who dances) a jazz variation of the two-step in which
    couples swing, balance, and twirl

jive¹ /jiev/ *n*
    (dancing or the energetic dance performed to) swing music

jive² *vt*
    to dance to or play jive

Joachim, Joseph /yoh'ahk(h)im, 'yohə,k(h)im/
    (1831–1907) Hungarian violinist and composer

jodel /'yohdl/ *vb*
    to yodel – **jodel** *n*

John, Elton /jon/
    né *Reginald Dwight* (born 1947) English rock singer

joint /joynt/ *n*
    a section of a woodwind instrument, esp a flute

Jones, Gwyneth /johnz/
    (born 1936) Welsh soprano

jongleur /ˌzhong'gluh/ *n*
    a wandering medieval musical entertainer whose skills
    included play-acting, tumbling, and conjuring

Joplin, Scott /'joplin/

(1868–1917) American pianist and composer of ragtime

Josquin Desprez /ˈzhoskan dayˈpray/

(c1440–1521) Northern French composer of sacred and
secular vocal music

jota /ˈhohtə, -ta/ *n*

(the music for) a Spanish folk dance in triple time
performed by a man and a woman to intricate castanet and
heel rhythms

Joyce, Eileen /joys/

(born 1912) Australian pianist

Jubilate /ˌjoohbiˈlahti/ *n*

(a musical setting of) the 100th psalm sung liturgically in
Catholic and Anglican churches

K

Kammer /'kamə/ *n*
chamber

Kapellmeister /ka'pel,miestə/ *n*
the director of a choir or orchestra (originally, of the choir
or orchestra of a royal or papal chapel)

Karajan, Herbert von /'karə,yan/
(born 1908) Austrian conductor

Karsavina, Tamara /kah'savənə/
(1885–1978) Russian dancer

Katchen, Julius /'kachən/
(1926–69) American pianist

Kaye, Danny /kay/
pseudonym of *David Daniel Kominski* (born 1913)
American actor and singer

kazoo /kə'zooh/ *n, pl* **kazoos**
an instrument consisting of a tube into which one sings or
hums to vibrate a membrane covering a side hole

Kelly, Gene /'keli/
(born 1912) American film actor, dancer, choreographer,
and director

Kempe, Rudolf /'kempə/
(1910–76) German conductor

Kempff, Wilhelm /kempf/
(born 1895) German pianist

Kenton, Stanley Newcomb /'kentən/
(1912–79) American bandleader and composer

Kern, Jerome David /kuhn/
(1885–1945) American composer

kettledrum /'ketl,drum/ *n*
a percussion instrument that consists of a hollow brass or
copper hemisphere with a parchment head whose tension

can be changed to vary the pitch

key /kee/ *n*

1a any of the levers of a keyboard instrument that is pressed by a finger or foot to actuate the mechanism and produce the notes

1b a lever that controls a vent in the side of a woodwind instrument or a valve in a brass instrument

2 a (particular) system of 7 notes based on their relationship to a tonic

3 characteristic style or tone – **keyed** *adj*, **keyless** *adj*

keyboard /-,bawd/ *n*

a bank of keys on an instrument (e g a piano) typically having 7 usu white and 5 raised usu black keys to the octave

key bugle *n*

any of a family of keyed wind instruments popular in the 19th c; *specif* a treble instrument of the ophicleide type

keynote /'key,noht/ *n*

the first and harmonically fundamental note of a scale

key signature *n*

the sharps or flats placed on the staff to indicate the key – see illustration

Khachaturian, Aram Ilych /,kachə'toori·ən/

(1903–78) Soviet composer; works include symphonies, concertos, ballets, and chamber, piano, and stage music

King, Hetty /king/

(1883–1972) English music-hall entertainer

Kirckman /'kuhkmən/

English firm of harpsichord and piano makers

klavier /'klavi·ə/ *n*

a clavier

Klemperer, Otto /'klempərə/

(1885–1973) German conductor and composer

Köchel, Ludwig von /'kuhkl/

(1800–77) Austrian musical biographer and cataloguer of

Major and Minor Key Signatures

 = Major   ● = Minor

Sharps

C   G   D   A   E
A   E   B   F♯   C♯

B   F♯   C♯
G♯   D♯   A♯

Flats

C   F   B♭   E♭   A♭
A   D   G   C   F

D♭   G♭   C♭
B♭   E♭   A♭

Mozart's works

Köchel number *n*
the number assigned to a work in Köchel's catalogue of
Mozart's music

Kodály, Zoltán /'koh,die/
(1882–1967) Hungarian composer of chamber, piano, vocal,
and choral music; collected Hungarian folk tunes

kolomyika /,kohloh'mi(yə)kə/ *n*
a quick Polish dance in duple time

Kostelanetz, André /kosteə'lahnets/
(1901–80) American (Russian-born) conductor

koto /'koh,toh/ *n, pl* **kotos**
a long Japanese instrument with a rectangular wooden body
and 13 silk strings

Koussevitzky, Serge /,koohsə'vitski(ə)/
Sergei Alexandrovitch (1874–1951) Russian-born conductor

kozachok /,kohzə'chok/ *n*
(the music, often in a minor key, for) a Cossack dance in
fairly quick duple time which gets faster as the dance
proceeds

Kraus, Lili /krows/
(born 1905) British (Hungarian-born) pianist

Kreisler, Fritz /'kriezlə/
(1875–1962) American (Austrian-born) violinist

Krips, Josef /krips/
(1902–74) Austrian conductor

krummhorn /'kroom,hawn/ *n*
a crumhorn

Kubelík, (Jeronym) Rafael /'koohbə,lik/
(born 1914) Czech conductor and composer

L

labial¹ /'laybi·əl/ *adj*
giving its tones from impact of an air current on a lip or liplike edge <*a ~ instrument like the flute*>

labial² *n*
a flue pipe

lacrimoso /ˌlakri'mohsoh, -zoh/ *adv or adj*
marked by a plaintive style

lah, la /lah/ *n*
the 6th note of the diatonic scale in solmization

Laine, Cleo /layn/
(born 1927) English jazz singer

Lalo, Edouard /'lahloh/
(1823–92) French composer

Lambert, Constant /'lambət/
(1905–51) English composer and conductor; works include *Rio Grande* for chorus, piano, and orchestra

lament /lə'ment/ *n*
a dirge, elegy

lamentoso /ˌlamən'tohsoh, -zoh/ *adv or adj*
in a plaintive or sad manner

lancers /'lahnsəz/ *n taking sing vb*
(the music for) a set of 5 quadrilles each in a different metre

ländler /'lentlə/ *n, pl* **ländler, ländlers**
(music for) an Austrian couple dance of rural origin in triple time that was a precursor of the waltz but slower and performed with stamping somewhat dragging steps

Landowska, Wanda Louise /lan'dofskə, -'dov-/
(1879–1959) Polish harpsichordist

langsam /'lang,zahm/ *adv or adj*
slowly, slow

largamente /ˌlahgə'mentay/ *adv or adj*

with slowness and breadth

larghetto /lah'getoh/ *n, adv, or adj, pl* **larghettos**
(a composition or movement that is) slower than andante but not as slow as largo

largo /'lahgoh/ *n, adv, or adj, pl* **largos**
(a movement to be) played in a very slow and broad manner

Larsson, Lars-Erik /'lahsən/
(born 1908) Swedish composer and conductor

Lassus, Orlande de /'lasəs/
Orlando di Lasso (1532–94) Franco-Flemish composer of sacred and secular vocal music

Lauder, Sir Harry /'lawdə/
né *MacLennan* (1870–1950) Scottish singer

Lawes, Henry /lawz/
(1596–1662) English composer, esp of songs and music for masques

Laye, Evelyn /lay/
(born 1900) English actress and singer

leader /'leedə/ *n*
1 *Br* the principal first violinist and usu assistant conductor of an orchestra
2 *NAm* a conductor – **leaderless** *adj*, **leadership** *n*

leading note *n*
the seventh note of a diatonic scale – called also SEVENTH, SUBTONIC

lebhaft /'layp,haft/ *adv or adj*
lively, vivace

Ledbetter, Huddie /'led,betə/
'*Leadbelly*' (1885–1949) American folksinger

ledger line, leger line /lejə/ *n*
a short line added above or below a staff to extend its range – see illustration at MUSIC

legatissimo /,legah'tisimoh/ *adv or adj*
in as smooth a manner as possible

legato /li'gahtoh/ *n, adv, or adj, pl* **legatos**
(a manner of performing or passage of music performed) in a smooth and connected manner

leggieramente /lə,jyeərah'mentay/ *adv*
lightly, delicately

leggiero /lə'jyeə,roh/ *adv or adj*
in a light and graceful manner

Lehár, Franz /'lay,hah/
(1870–1948) Austrian (Hungarian-born) composer, esp of operettas (e g *The Merry Widow*)

Lehmann, Lotte /'laymən/
(1888–1976) German soprano

Leinsdorf, Erich /'lients,dawf, 'lienz-/
(born 1912) American (Austrian-born) conductor

leitmotiv, leitmotif /'lietmoh,teef/ *n*
a theme in an opera or a symphonic poem that denotes an idea, person, or situation

Lennon, John Ono /'lenən/
(1940–80) English pop musician; member of the *Beatles*

lento /'lentoh/ *adv or adj*
slow

Leoncavallo, Ruggero /,lay,onkə'valoh/
(1857–1919) Italian librettist and composer; works include the opera *Pagliacci*

Leonhardt, Gustav /'luyon,haht/
(born 1928) Dutch harpsichordist

Leppard, Raymond /'lepahd/
(born 1927) English conductor and harpsichordist

Leschetizky, Theodor /,leshə'titski/
(1830–1915) Polish pianist, piano teacher, and composer

Lewis, John Aaron /'looh·is/
(born 1920) American jazz composer and pianist

libretto /li'bretoh/ *n, pl* **librettos, libretti** /-ti/
(the book containing) the text of an opera, oratorio or other

large-scale vocal work – **librettist** *n*

Lichine, David /li'sheen/
(1910–72) Soviet ballet dancer and choreographer

lied /leed/ *n*, *pl* **lieder** /'leedə/
a German song; *esp* a 19th-c setting for solo voice and piano of a lyrical poem

Lifar, Serge /'li,fah, li'fah/
(born 1905) Russian dancer

lift /lift/ *n*
the lifting up of a dancer usu by her partner

ligature /'ligəchə/ *n*
1 a slur
2 a flexible metal band with adjusting screws that holds in place the reed of a single reed woodwind instrument (e g a clarinet)

Ligeti, György /li'geti/
(born 1923) Austrian (Hungarian-born) composer

light opera *n*
an operetta

limbo /'limboh/ *n*, *pl* **limbos**
a West Indian acrobatic dance that involves bending over backwards and passing under a low horizontal pole

Lind, Jenny /lind/
'*Johanna Maria*'; the '*Swedish Nightingale*' (1820–87) Swedish soprano

line /lien/ *n*
any of the horizontal parallel strokes on a staff on or between which notes are placed – compare SPACE; see illustration at MUSIC

lip /lip/ *n*
1 an embouchure
2 the edge in a flue pipe (e g in a pipe organ) across which a current of air is forced causing a wave motion in the air within the pipe that produces a note

lipping /ˈliping/ *n*
an embouchure

l'istesso tempo /leeˌstesoh ˈtempoh/ *adv or adj*
in the same tempo as before

Liszt, Franz /list/
(1811–86) Hungarian pianist and composer of symphonies, symphonic poems, piano music, and sacred works

literature /ˈlit(ə)rəchə/ *n*
the body of compositions <*the piano ~ of Brahms*>

Litolff, Henry Charles /ˈlitolf/
(1818–91) French composer and pianist

liturgy /ˈlitəji/ *n*
1 *often cap* the form of service used in the celebration of Communion, esp in the Orthodox church
2 a prescribed form of public worship – **liturgical** *adj*, **liturgically** *adv*

Lloyd, Marie /loyd/
née *Matilda Wood* (1870–1922) English music-hall entertainer

Lloyd Webber, Andrew /ˌloydˈwebə/
(born 1948) English composer

Locke, Matthew /lok/
(?1621–77) English composer

loco /ˈlohkoh/ *adv or adj*
in the register as written – compare OTTAVA

Loewe, (Johann) Carl (Gottfried) /ˈluhvə/
(1796–1869) German conductor, pianist, singer, and composer, esp of vocal works (e g *Der Erlkönig*)

Loewe, Frederick /ˈloh(i)/
(born 1904) American (Austrian-born) composer

Lomax, Alan /ˈlohˌmaks/
son of John, (born 1915) American folksinger

Lomax, John Avery
(1872–1948) American folklorist

lontano /lon'tahnoh/ *adv or adj*
as from a distance

loud pedal *n*
misleading term for the sustaining pedal on a piano

Loughran, James /'lokrən/
(born 1931) Scottish conductor

loure /'loo(ə)r/ *n*
1 a dance in slow triple or sextuple time; *also* the music for such a dance
2 a kind of bagpipe

low /loh/ *adj*
1 *of sound* not shrill or loud; soft
2 depressed in pitch <*a ~ note*> – **lowness** *n*

low-pitched *adj*
of sound not shrill; deep

Ludwig, Christa /,lood'vik(h)/
(born 1924) German mezzo-soprano

lullaby /'luləbie/ *n*
a song to quieten children or lull them to sleep

Lully, Jean-Baptiste /looh'li/
(1632–87) French (Italian-born) composer, esp of operas and ballets

lunga pausa /,loohngə 'powzə/ *n*
a long pause

lusingando /,loohseen'gandoh/ *adv or adj*
in a coaxing manner

lute /looht/ *n*
a stringed instrument with a large pear-shaped body, a neck with a fretted fingerboard, and pairs of strings tuned in unison

lutenist /'loohtinist/ , **lutanist** /-tən-/ *n*
a lute player

Lutoslawski, Witold /,loohtoh'slafski/
(born 1913) Polish composer

Lutyens, (Agnes) Elisabeth /'lutshənz/
  daughter of architect Sir Edwin, (1906–83) English
  composer, esp of orchestral and chamber music; exponent
  of twelve-note music

lydian mode /lidi·ən/ *n, often cap L*
  an authentic mode which may be represented on the white
  keys of the piano on a scale from F to F

Lympany, Moura /'lim,pəni/
  (born 1916) English pianist

Lynn, Dame Vera /lin/
  (born 1917) English singer

lyre /'lie·ə/ *n*
  a stringed instrument of the harp family used by the ancient
  Greeks esp to accompany song and recitation

lyric /'lirik/ *adj*
  suitable for being set to music and sung

lyricism /'lirisiz(ə)m/ *n*
  a directly personal and intense style or quality in an art

lyrics *n pl*
  the words of a popular song – **lyricist, lyrist** *n*

M

Maazel, Lorin /mah'zel/
(born 1930) American conductor

McCartney, Paul /mə'kaht,ni/
(born 1942) English pop musician; member of the *Beatles*

McCormack, John /mə'kawmək, -mik/
(1884–1945) Irish tenor

MacDowell, Edward Alexander /mək'dow(ə)l/
(1860–1908) American composer and pianist

Machaut, Guillaume de /'mashoh/
(c1300–1377) French composer

machine head *n*
any of the structures in the head of a guitar or related
instrument through which the strings are threaded and
which connect with the tuning pegs via cogs

Mackenzie, Sir Alexander Campbell /mə'kenzi/
(1847–1935) British composer and conductor

Mackerras, Sir Charles /mə'kerəs/
(born 1925) Australian conductor

McKie, Sir William Neil /mə'kie/
(born 1901) Australian organist

MacMillan, Kenneth /mək'milən/
(born 1929) British dancer and choreographer

Maconchy, Elizabeth /mə'konki/
(born 1907) English composer

madrigal /'madrig(ə)l/ *n*
1 an unaccompanied and often complex secular song for
several voices
2 a part-song; *esp* a glee – **madrigalian** *adj*

maestoso /mie'stohsoh, -zoh/ *n, adv, or adj*
(a composition or movement to be played) in a majestic and
stately style and usu in moderate tempo

maestro /'miestroh/ *n, pl* **maestros, maestri** /-tri/
a master in an art; *esp* an eminent composer, conductor, or
teacher of music

Magnificat /mag'nifikat/ *n*
(a musical setting of) the canticle of the Virgin Mary in
Luke 1:46–55 that forms part of the services of *Vespers* and
Evensong

Mahler, Gustav /'mahlə/
(1860–1911) Austrian conductor and composer; works
include 10 symphonies, some with vocal parts, and songs

major¹ /'mayjə/ *adj*
1 *esp of a scale or mode* having semitones between the third
and fourth and the seventh and eighth degrees
2 being or based on a (specified) major scale <*in a ~ key*>
<*a piece in D ~*>
3 being an interval (equivalent to that) between the first and
the second, third, sixth, or seventh degree of a major scale –
compare AUGMENTED, DIMINISHED, MINOR, PERFECT
4 *of a chord* having an interval of a major third between the
root and the next note above it

major² *n*
a major interval, scale, key, or mode

majorette /,mayjə'ret/ *n*
a girl or woman who twirls a baton and accompanies a
marching band

malagueña /,malə'gaynyə, ,mol-, -gway-/ *n*
1 a folk tune native to Malaga, Spain, which is similar to a
fandango and to which verses are sung
2 a Spanish couple dance similar to a fandango

mallet /'malit/ *n*
a light hammer with a small rounded or spherical usu
padded head used in playing certain instruments (e g a
vibraphone)

mambo /'mamboh/ *n, pl* **mambos**

(the music for) a ballroom dance of Haitian origin that
resembles the rumba – **mambo** *vi*

mancando /man'kandoh/ , **mancante** /-'kantay/ *adv or adj*
dying away

manchega /man'chaygə/ *n*
a bright and lively seguidilla danced in the province of La
Mancha

mandolin *also* **mandoline** /ˌmandə'lin/ *n*
an instrument of the lute family with a fretted neck

ma non troppo /ma ˌnon 'tropoh/ *adv or adj*
but not too much – used to qualify a direction

manual /'manyooəl/ *n*
a keyboard for the hands; *specif* any of the several
keyboards of an organ that control separate divisions of the
instrument

maraca /mə'rakə/ *n*
a dried gourd filled with seeds or a rattle like a gourd that is
used as a rhythm instrument and is usu played as one of a
pair

marc. *adv or adj*
marcato

marcato /mah'kahtoh/ *adv or adj*
with strong accentuation

march /mahch/ *n*
a composition that is usu in duple or quadruple time with a
strongly accentuated beat and is designed or suitable to
accompany marching

marimba /mə'rimbə/ *n*
a percussion instrument resembling a large xylophone

Markova, Dame Alicia /ˌmah'kohvə/
Lilian Alicia Marks (born 1910) English dancer

martellato[1] /ˌmaht(ə)'lahtoh/ *adv or adj*
hammered, i.e. detached and strongly accented – used as a
direction to players of bowed instruments; compare

DÉTACHÉ

martellato² *n*

martellato technique, notes, or effect

marziale /ˌmahtziˈahlay/ *adv or adj*

in a martial manner

Mascagni, Pietro /masˈkah.nyi/

(1863–1945) Italian composer, esp of opera; works include *Cavalleria Rusticana*

masculine /ˈmaskyoolin/ *adj*

having the final chord occurring on a strong beat –

masculinely *adv*

masked ball *n*

a ball at which the participants wear masks

masque /mahsk/ *n*

a short allegorical English stage entertainment of the 16th and 17th c that developed round a masked dance

mass /mas/ *n*

1 *cap* the liturgy of the Eucharist

2 a musical setting, usu in 5 sections, for the ordinary of the Mass

Massenet, Jules Émile Frédéric /ˈmas(ə)ˌnay/

(1842–1912) French composer; works include operas (e g *Manon*), ballets, choral and orchestral music, and some 200 songs

mässig /ˈmaysikh/ *adv or adj*

moderato

Massine, Léonide /maˈseen/

(1896–1979) American (Russian-born) dancer and choreographer

master class *n*

a class in which an eminent musician teaches advanced pupils

Mastersinger /ˈmahstəˌsingə/ *n*

a member of any of various German guilds formed from the

14th to the 17th c by working men and craftsmen to continue the art of the Minnesingers for the cultivation of poetry and music

Mathieson, Muir /ˈmathisən/
(1911–1975) Scottish composer and conductor

Matthews, Denis /ˈmath‚yoohz/
(born 1919) English pianist

maxixe /məˈsheesh(ə)/ *n*
a ballroom dance of Brazilian origin that resembles the two-step in rhythm and action

mazurka *also* **mazourka** /məˈzuhkə/ *n*
(music for, or in the rhythm of) a Polish folk dance in moderate triple time with the second beat of the bar accentuated

me, mi /mee/ *n*
the 3rd note of the diatonic scale in solmization

measure /ˈmezhə/ *n*
1 a (slow and stately) dance
2 time
3 *NAm* the notes and rests that form a bar of music

mediant /ˈmeedi‚ənt/ *n*
the 3rd note of a diatonic scale – called also THIRD

mediation /‚meedi'aysh(ə)n/ *n*
the cadence between the 2 reciting notes in a Gregorian psalm tone or an Anglican chant

medley /ˈmedli/ *n*
a composition made up of a series of songs or short pieces

Mehta, Zubin /ˈmaytə/
(born 1936) Indian conductor

Meistersinger /ˈmiestə‚singə, -zingə/ *n*
a Mastersinger

Melba, Dame Nellie /ˈmelbə/
née *Helen Porter Mitchell* (1861–1931) Australian soprano

Melchior, Lauritz Lebrecht Hommel /ˈmelki·aw(ə)/

(1890–1973) American (Danish-born) tenor

melisma /mə'lizmə/ *n, pl* **melismata** /-mətə/
a group of notes or tones sung on 1 syllable, esp in plainsong, for display or for greater expression – **melismatic** *adj*

mellophone /'melə,fohn/ *n*
a circular valved brass instrument with a range similar to that of the French horn

Mellotron /'melə,tron/ *trademark*
– used for an electronic keyboard instrument in which the sound source is a prerecorded tape

melodeon, melodion /mə'lohdi·ən/ *n*
a reed organ in which the air is drawn through the reeds by suction bellows

melodic /mə'lodik/ *adj*
1 of or forming melody
2 melodious – **melodically** *adv*

melodious /mə'lohdi·əs/ *adj*
of or producing (a pleasing) melody – **melodiously** *adv*, **melodiousness** *n*

melodist /'melədist/ *n*
1 a singer
2 a composer of melodies

melody /'melədi/ *n*
1 a succession of single notes of different pitches organized as an aesthetic whole; a tune
2 the chief part in a harmonic composition
3 a line as it appears on the staff when viewed horizontally

Mendelssohn(-Bartholdy), (Jakob Ludwig) Felix /'mendlsən,bah't(h)awldi/
grandson of the philosopher Moses Mendelssohn, (1809–47) German composer, pianist, and conductor; works include chamber and orchestral music (e g the overtures *The Hebrides or Fingal's Cave* and *A Midsummer Night's*

Dream), choral music (e g the oratorio *Elijah*) and songs, and piano and organ pieces

meno /'maynoh/ *adv or adj*
less <~ *mosso*>

meno mosso /'mosoh/ *adv or adj*
less lively; slower

Menotti, Gian-Carlo /mə'noti/
(born 1911) American (Italian-born) composer, esp of opera

Menuhin, Yehudi /'menyooh·in/
(born 1916) American violinist

Mercer, Johnny /'muhsə/
(1909–76) American singer and songwriter

Merman, Ethel /'muhmən/
(born 1909) American singer and actress

messa di voce /,mesa ,dee 'vohchay/ *n, adv, or adj*
– used as a direction in singing to indicate a crescendo and diminuendo on a long-held note

Messiaen, Olivier (Eugène Prosper Charles) /me'syanh/
(born 1908) French organist and composer of choral, organ, and orchestral music with strong religious influence

mesto /'mestoh/ *adv or adj*
sad and pensive in nature

metre , *NAm chiefly* **meter** /'meetə/ *n*
a basic recurrent rhythmical pattern of accents and beats per bar

metronome /'metrə,nohm/ *n*
an instrument designed to mark exact time by a regularly repeated tick – **metronomic** *adj*

Meyerbeer, Giacomo /'mie·ə,beə/
né *Jakob Liebmann Meyer Beer* (1791–1864) German composer, esp of opera

mezza voce /,metsə 'vohchi/ *adv or adj*
with medium or half volume of tone

mezzo /'metsoh/ , **mezzo-soprano** n, pl **mezzos,
mezzo-sopranos**
(a singer with) a woman's voice with a range between that
of the soprano and contralto
mezzo forte /'fawtay/ adj or adv
moderately loud
mezzo piano /pi'ahnoh/ adj or adv
moderately soft
mf adj or adv
mezzo forte
mi /mee/ n
me
Michelangeli, Arturo Benedetti /ˌmishel'anjəli/
(born 1920) Italian pianist
microtone /'miekroh,tohn/ n
an interval smaller than a semitone – **microtonally** adv,
microtonal adj, **microtonality** n
middle C n
the note designated by the first ledger line below the treble
staff and the first above the bass staff and having a
standardized frequency of 261.63 Hertz
Milhaud, Darius /mi'yoh/
(1892–1974) French composer
miniature score n
a full score of pocket size
minim /'minim/ n
a note with the time value of 2 crotchets or half a semibreve
– see illustration at NOTE – **minim** adj
minim rest n
a rest of the same time value as a minim
Minnelli, Liza /mi'neli/
(born 1946) American singer and actress
Minnesinger /'miniˌsing-ə/ n
a member of a guild of German lyric poets and musicians of

the 12th to the 14th c

minor¹ /'mienə/ adj

1 *esp of a scale or mode* having semitones between the second and third, fifth and sixth, and sometimes seventh and eighth steps

2 being or based on a (specified) minor scale <*in a ~ key*> <*a piece in A ~*>

3 being an interval less by a semitone than a corresponding major interval – compare AUGMENTED, DIMINISHED, MAJOR, PERFECT

4 *of a chord* having an interval of a minor third between the root and the next note above it

minor² n

a minor interval, scale, key, or mode

minstrel /'minstrəl/ n

a medieval singer, poet, or musical entertainer

minstrelsy /-si/ n

1 the singing and playing of a minstrel

2 *taking sing or pl vb* a body of minstrels

3 songs or poems (composed or performed by minstrels)

minuet /ˌminyoo'et/ n

(music for or in the rhythm of) a slow graceful dance in triple time, commonly followed by a second minuet, the trio, after which the first is repeated

misterioso /miˌsteəri'ohsoh, -zoh/ adv or adj

in a mysterious manner

misura /mi'zoorə/ n

measure, tempo <*senza ~*>

mixolydian mode /ˌmiksoh'lidi·ən/ n, often cap 1st M

an authentic mode which may be represented on the white keys of the piano on a scale from G to G

mixture stop, mixture n

a pipe-organ stop having more than one pipe for each key

mod /mod/ n

a Gaelic competitive festival of the arts, esp singing and
recitation, held in Scotland

modal /'mohdl/ *adj*

of or being (in) a mode; *specif* being in one of the church
modes rather than a major or minor key – **modally** *adv*

mode /mohd/ *n*

1 an arrangement of the 8 diatonic notes of an octave in any
of several fixed schemes which use different patterns of
whole tones and semitones between successive notes

2 a rhythmical scheme, esp in 13th and 14th-c music

moderato /ˌmodə'rahtoh/ *adv or adj*

in a moderate tempo

modulate /'modyoolayt/ *vb*

vt to vary in tone; make tuneful <~ *one's voice*> ~
vi to pass by regular chord or melodic progression from one
key or tonality into another – **modulator** *n*, **modulatory** *adj*

modulation /ˌmodyoo'laysh(ə)n/ *n*

a change from one key or tonality to another by regular
melodic or chord progression

Moeran, Ernest John /'mawˌrən/ *n*

(1894–1950) English composer

moll /mol/ *adj*

in the minor mode; minor <*G* ~>

molto /'moltoh/ *adv*

much, very <~ *sostenuto*>

monochord /'monəˌkawd/ *n*

an instrument consisting of a single string used for
measuring and demonstrating the mathematical relations of
notes

monody /'monədi/ *n*

the monophonic style of music (e g in 17th-c Italian opera);
also a composition in this style

monophonic /ˌmonoh'fonik/ *adj*

1 having a single melodic line with little or no

accompaniment

2 of or being sound reproduction or a system for recording or reproducing sound that uses only one electrical channel between the source of the signal and its final point of use

monophony /mə'nofəni/ *n*

monophonic music

monotone /'monə,tohn/ *n*

a single unvaried note; *specif* a reciting note in Gregorian chant

monotonous /mə'not(ə)nəs/ *adj*

uttered or sounded in 1 unvarying tone – **monotonously** *adv*, **monotonousness, monotony** *n*

montage /monh'tahzh/ *n*

an artistic composition made from different materials combined or juxtaposed

Monteux, Pierre /mon'tuh/

(1875–1964) American (French-born) conductor

Monteverdi, Claudio Giovanni Antonio /ˌmontə'veədi/

(1567–1643) Italian composer, esp of operas, madrigals, and church music

Montgomery, (Robert) Bruce /mən(t)'gom(ə)ri/

(1921–78) English composer

Moog /moohg/ **, Moog synthesizer** *trademark*

– a musical synthesizer named after its inventor, Robert Moog

Moore, Gerald /'maw(ə)/

(born 1899) English pianist, noted as an accompanist

mordent /'mawd(ə)nt/ *n*

(a symbol on the staff indicating) an ornament made by a quick alternation of a principal note with either of the immediately adjacent notes – see illustration at DIRECTION

morendo /mə'rendoh/ *adv or adj*

dying away

moresca /mə'reskə/ **, moresco** /-koh/ **, morisco** *n* a Moorish dance

Morison, Elsie /'morisən/
(born 1924) Australian soprano

Morley, Thomas /'mawli/
(c1557–1602) English composer

morris dance /'moris/ *n*
any of several traditional English dances that are performed
by groups of people wearing costumes to which small bells
are attached – **morris dancer** *n*

Morton, Jelly Roll /'mawt(ə)n/
né *Ferdinand Joseph La Menthe Morton* (1885–1941)
American jazz pianist, bandleader, and composer

mosso /'mohsoh/ *adj or adv*
animated

motet /moh'tet/ *n*
a usu unaccompanied sacred choral composition in
contrapuntal style

motif /moh'teef/ *n*
a recurrent phrase, figure or theme that is developed
through the course of a composition

motion /'mohsh(ə)n/ *n*
melodic change of pitch

motive /'mohtiv/ *n*
a motif

moto /'mohtoh, 'mohdoh/ *n*
movement with regard to tempo

moto perpetuo /,mohtoh pə'petyooh,oh/ *n*
a composition having the same rapid motion from beginning
to end

mouth organ *n*
a harmonica

mouthpiece *n*
1 a structure that serves as a mouth <~ *of a reed organ
pipe*>

2a a part of an instrument to which the mouth is applied

2b a part of an instrument that goes into the mouth

mouth pipe *n*

1 an organ flue pipe

2 the pipe in a bagpipe through which the air is blown

3 the section of a musical wind instrument into which the mouthpiece is inserted

movement /'moohvmənt/ *n*

a unit or division having its own key, rhythmic structure, and themes and forming a separate part of an extended composition

movimento /ˌmohvi'mentoh/ *n*

tempo

Mozart, Wolfgang Amadeus /'moht,saht/

(1756–91) Austrian composer; famous as child prodigy; his many works include nearly 50 symphonies, operas (e g *The Marriage of Figaro* and *Don Giovanni*), piano concertos, string quartets, violin sonatas, and much other music – **Mozartean, Mozartian** *adj*

mp adj or adv

mezzo piano

ms *n, often cap M&S*

manuscript

muiñeira , muñeira /mooh'nyeərə/ *n*

a Spanish song and dance in sextuple time

Münch, Charles /'moohnch/

(1891–1968) French conductor

murciana /ˌmuhshee'anə/ *n*

a fandango of Murcia, Spain

Murrill, Herbert /'muril/

(1909–52) English composer

musette /myooh'zet/ *n*

1 a small bagpipe having a soft sweet tone

2 a quiet pastoral air that often has a drone bass and is

adapted to the musette

3 a gavotte danced to the tune of a musette

Musgrave, Thea /'muz,grayv/
(born 1928) Scottish composer, esp of orchestral and chamber music, songs, and much incidental music

music /'myoohzik/ *n*
1 the science or art of ordering notes or sounds in succession and combination to produce a composition having unity and continuity
2 vocal, instrumental, or mechanical sounds having rhythm, melody, or harmony
3 the score of a composition set down on paper – see illustration

musical¹ /'myoohzikl/ *adj*
1 having the pleasing harmonious qualities of music
2 having an interest in or talent for music
3 set to or accompanied by music
4 of music, musicians, or music lovers – **musically** *adv*, **musicality** *n*

musical² *n*
a film or theatrical production that consists of songs, dances, and dialogue based on a unifying plot

musical box , *chiefly NAm* **music box** *n*
a container enclosing an apparatus that reproduces music mechanically when activated

musical comedy *n*
1 a musical; *esp* one of a sentimental or humorous nature
2 an esp American operetta popular during the late 19th and early 20th c

music drama *n*
Wagnerian opera in which equal importance is given to the drama and the music

musician /myooh'zish(ə)n/ *n*
a composer, conductor, or performer of music; *esp* an

First bars of Schubert's *Gute Nacht*

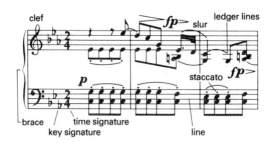

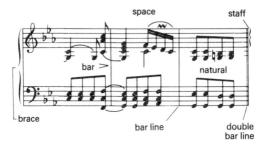

Clefs

G or treble clef

F or bass clef

alto clef

tenor clefs

The C clef is called the alto clef or the tenor clef, depending on where it is placed on the staff. The positions of middle C on the alto and tenor clefs are shown.

Accidentals

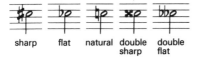

sharp   flat   natural   double sharp   double flat

Accidentals are notes that are outside the key indicated by the key signature.

instrumentalist – **musicianship** n

musicology /ˌmyoohzi'koləji/ n

the study of music as a branch of knowledge or field of research – **musicologist** n, **musicological** adj

music theatre n

a modern small-scale musical drama that differs from conventional opera esp in not requiring the facilities of a fully equipped opera house

musique concrète /mooh,zeek kong'kret/ n

a montage of recorded natural sounds (e g voices, traffic noise, and bird calls) arbitrarily modified and arranged

Mussorgsky, Modest Petrovich /moo'sawgski/

(1839–81) Russian composer; works include operas (e g *Boris Godunov*), orchestral and piano music, and songs

muta /'moohtə/ n

a change – used as a direction in ensemble music for various instruments (e g timpani) to change tuning preparatory to a change in key

mutation stop n

a pipe-organ stop sounding pitches other than those indicated by the notes or one of their octaves (e g a fifth and a twelfth) – compare FOUNDATION STOP

mute[1] /myooht/ n

a device that may be attached to an instrument (e g a violin or trumpet) to reduce, soften, or muffle its tone

mute[2] vt

to muffle or reduce the sound of

muted adj

provided with or produced or modified by the use of a mute – **mutedly** adv

Muzak /'myoohzak/ trademark

– used for recorded background music played in public places

N

nachtanz /'nahkh,tahnts/ *n*

the second of two dances in a contrasted pair (e g a pavane and galliard)

natural¹ /'nachərəl/ *adj*

1 (containing only notes that are) neither sharp nor flat

2 having the pitch modified by the natural sign

natural² *n*

1 **natural, natural sign** a sign placed on the staff to nullify the effect of a preceding sharp or flat – see illustration at MUSIC

2 a note affected by a natural sign

neck /nek/ *n*

the part of a stringed instrument extending from the body and supporting the fingerboard and strings

Neel, Louis Boyd /neel/

(1905–81) English conductor

neoclassic /,neeoh'klasik/ , **neoclassical** /-kl/ *adj*

of or constituting a revival or adaptation of the classical, esp in literature, music, art, or architecture – **neoclassicism** *n*, **neoclassicist** *n or adj*

Neuschel /'noy,shəl/

German family of brass instrument makers responsible for the development of the trombone: esp **Hans** (died 1533)

new wave *n, often cap N&W*

a style of rock music that developed from punk rock and is usu more complex musically while retaining an emphasis on social comment

nickelodeon /,nik(ə)l'ohdi·ən/ *n*

a jukebox

Nielsen, Carl August /'ne(ə)lsən/

(1865–1931) Danish composer

Nijinska, Bronislava /nəˈzhinskə, -ˈjin-/
sister of Waslaw, (1891–1972) Russian dancer and
choreographer

Nijinsky, Waslaw /nəˈzhinski, -ˈjin-/
(1890–1950) Russian dancer

Nilsson, Birgit /ˈnilsən/
(born 1918) Swedish soprano

ninth /nienth/ *n*
1 (a chord containing) an interval of an octave and a second
2 the note separated by this interval from a lower note –
ninth *adj*

nobilmente /ˌnohbilˈmentay/ *adv or adj*
in a noble manner

nocturne /ˈnoktuhn/ *n*
a work of art dealing with evening or night; *esp* a short,
lyrical piano piece

nonet /ˌnoˈnet/ *n*
(a musical composition for) 9 instruments, voices, or
composers

non tanto /ˌnon ˈtantoh/ *adj or adv*
not so much

non troppo /ˌnon ˈtropoh/ *adv or adj*
without excess

note /noht/ *n*
1 a sound having a definite pitch
2 a written symbol used to indicate duration and pitch of a
tone by its shape and position on the staff – see illustration
3 a key of a piano, organ, etc

note-row /roh/ *n*
the 12 chromatic notes of the octave placed in a chosen
fixed order that forms the basis of the material in a
twelve-note composition

novelette /ˌnovlˈet/ *n*
a romantic movement written in free form

Notes and Rests

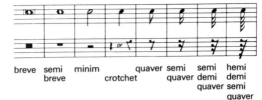

| breve | semi breve | minim | | crotchet | quaver | semi quaver | semi demi quaver | hemi demi semi quaver |

Values

Each note is played or sung exactly half as long as the one in the row above.

Dots

When a note has a dot placed after it, it is held for exactly half as long again: $\text{♩.} = \text{♩} + \text{♪}$

When a note has a double dot placed after it, it is held for exactly three quarters as long again: $\text{♩..} = \text{♩} + \text{♪} + \text{♪}$

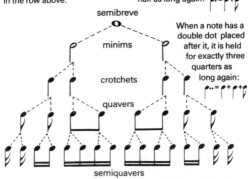

semibreve

minims

crotchets

quavers

semiquavers

Novello, Ivor /nə'veloh/
pseudonym of *David Ivor Davies* (1893–1951) Welsh actor, composer, songwriter, and dramatist

number opera *n*
an opera written in numbers, or self-contained pieces of music (e g arias, duets, and choruses), separated by recitative or spoken dialogue. This form was prevalent until the middle of the 19th c when it was replaced by more continuous writing and is today usu found only in musicals.

Nunc Dimittis /ˌnoongk di'mitis, ˌnungk/ *n*
(a musical setting of) the canticle of Simeon in Luke 2:29–32 that forms part of the services of *Compline* and *Evensong*

Nureyev, Rudolph Hametovich /nyooh'rayef/
(born 1938) British (Russian-born) ballet dancer and choreographer

nut /nut/ *n*
1 the ridge in a stringed instrument (e g a violin) over which the strings pass on the upper end of the fingerboard
2 the device at the heel of a string-player's bow which alters the tension of the hairs

O

obbligato¹ /ˌobli'gahtoh/ *adj*
not to be omitted

obbligato² *n, pl* **obbligatos** *also* **obbligati** /-ti/
an elaborate, esp melodic, accompaniment, usu played by a
single instrument

obertass, obertas /oh'beətas/ *n*
a Polish round dance in quick triple time

oboe /'oh,boh/ *n*
1 a double-reed woodwind instrument with a conical tube
and a usual range from B flat below middle C upwards for
about 2 octaves
2 an organ reed stop that gives a tone resembling that of an
oboe – **oboist** *n*

oboe d'amore /dah'mawray/ *n*
a mezzo-soprano oboe having a pear-shaped bell and
sombre tone and used esp in Baroque music

ocarina /ˌokə'reenə/ *n*
a simple wind instrument with an oval body

Ockeghem, Johannes /'okəgem/
(*c*1410–97) Franco-Flemish composer

octave /'oktiv, 'oktayv/ *n*
1 (the combination of 2 notes at) an interval of 8 diatonic
degrees
2 a note separated from a lower note by this interval
3 the whole series of notes or piano, organ, etc keys within
this interval that form the unit of the modern scale

octet /ok'tet/ *n*
(a composition for) 8 instruments, voices, or performers

Offenbach, Jacques /'ofən,bahkh/
(1819–80) French composer, esp of light operas and
operettas

off-key *adj*

varying in pitch from the proper tone of a melody

Ogdon, John Andrew Howard /'ogdən/

(born 1937) English pianist and composer

Oistrakh, David Fyodorovich /'oy,strahk/

(1908–74) Russian violinist

one-step *n*

(a piece of music used for) a ballroom dance marked by
quick walking steps – **one-step** *vi*

open /'ohp(ə)n/ *adj*

1 *of a string on an instrument* not stopped by the finger
2 *of a note* produced on an instrument without fingering the
strings, valves, slides, or keys – **open** *adv*

opera /'oprə/ *n*

1 (the performance of or score for) a drama set to music and
made up of vocal pieces with orchestral accompaniment and
usu other orchestral music (e g an overture)
2 the branch of the arts concerned with such works
3 a company performing operas – **operatic** *adj*, **operatically**
adv

opéra ballet *n*

a stage work in which singing and dancing are of equal
importance, first produced in France in the 17th and 18th c

opéra bouffe /,op(ə)rə 'boohf/ *n*

light, satirical opera

opera buffa /'boohfə/ *n*

comic opera, esp of a form popular in Italy in the 18th c

opéra comique /ko'meek/ *n*

opera with spoken dialogue and often, but not necessarily,
of a comical nature

opera semiseria /semi'sayree·ə/ *n*

opera combining elements of both tragedy and comedy

opera seria /'siəri·ə/ *n*

an 18th-c opera with a heroic or legendary subject

operetta /ˌopəˈretə/ *n*
a usu romantic light-hearted opera with spoken dialogue, songs, and dances – also called LIGHT OPERA – **operettist** *n*

ophicleide /ˈofiklied/ *n*
a keyed brass orchestral instrument superseded at the end of the 19th c by the tuba

opus /ˈohpəs/ *n, pl* **opera** /ˈop(ə)rə/ *also* **opuses**
a composition or set of compositions, usu numbered in the order of publication

oratorio /ˌorəˈtawrioh/ *n, pl* **oratorios**
a choral work based usu on a religious subject and composed chiefly of recitatives, arias, and choruses without action or scenery

orchestra /ˈawkistrə/ *n*
a group of musicians including esp string players organized to perform ensemble music

orchestral /awˈkestrəl/ *adj*
of or composed for an orchestra – **orchestrally** *adv*

orchestral score *n*
the full score of an orchestral work

orchestrate /ˈawkiˌstrayt/ *vt*
1 to compose or arrange (music) for an orchestra
2 to provide with orchestration <~ *a ballet*> – **orchestrator** *n*

orchestration /ˌawkiˈstraysh(ə)n/ *n*
(the style of) the arrangement of music for performance by an orchestra

ordinary /ˈawdn(ə)ri, ˈawd(ə)nri/ *n, often cap*
the invariable parts of the Mass. In settings for chorus these usu comprise the *Kyrie*, *Gloria in excelsis Deo*, *Credo*, *Sanctus* (including *Benedictus*), and *Agnus Dei* – compare PROPER

Orff, Carl /ˈaw(ə)f/
(1895–1982) German composer; works include choral

music, esp the scenic cantata *Carmina Burana*, operas, and
orchestral music

organ /'awgən/ *n*

1 a wind instrument consisting of sets of pipes made to
sound by compressed air and controlled by keyboards; *also*
an electronic keyboard instrument producing a sound
approximating to that of an organ

2 a reed organ

3 any of various similar cruder instruments – **organist** *n*

organ-grinder *n*

an itinerant street musician who operates a barrel organ

Ormandy, Eugene /'awmǝndi/

(1899–1985) American (Hungarian-born) conductor

ornament /'awnǝmǝnt/ *n*

an embellishing note not belonging to the essential harmony
or melody – see illustration at DIRECTION

ornamentation /ˌawnǝmǝn'taysh(ǝ)n/ *n*

the art of decorating or embellishing a melody that was
widely and freely practised by musicians, esp in the 17th and
18th c, but is today restricted to the use of conventionalized
ornaments and graces

ossia /oh'siǝ/ *conj*

or else – used to indicate an alternative and usu simpler
form of a passage

ostinato /ˌosti'nahtoh/ *n, pl* **ostinatos**

a figure repeated persistently at the same pitch throughout a
composition

ottava /oh'tahvǝ/ *n, adv, or adj*

(a symbol placed above a passage to be played) at an octave
higher or lower than written – see illustration at DIRECTION

ottava bassa *adj, adv, or n*

(at) an octave lower than printed

overtone /'ohvǝˌtohn/ *n*

any of the higher harmonics produced simultaneously with

the fundamental in a complex note – called also PARTIAL, UPPER PARTIAL

overture /ˈohvətyooə, -chə/ n

1 the orchestral introduction to a musical dramatic work

2 an orchestral concert piece in a single movement

Ozawa, Seiji /ohˈzahwə/

(born 1935) Japanese conductor

P

p adv or adj
  piano

Pachelbel, Johann /'pakl,bel/
  (1653–1706) German organist and composer of keyboard,
  choral, and vocal works

Paderewski, Ignace Jan /,padə'refski/
  (1860–1941) Polish pianist and composer

paean /'pee·ən/ *n*
  a joyously exultant song or hymn of praise, tribute,
  thanksgiving, or triumph

Paganini, Nicolò /,pagə'neeni/
  (1782–1840) Italian violinist

palais /'palay, 'pali/ , **palais de dance** /~ də 'donhs/ *n*
  a public dance hall

Palestrina, Giovanni Pierluigi da /,palə'streenə/
  (1526?–94) Italian composer, esp of contrapuntal sacred
  choral music

pallet /'palət/ *n*
  a hinged valve on a pipe organ to admit or release
  compressed air : e g
  a a valve opened by a key to admit wind to a groove under
  the pipes
  b a waste valve to release surplus air from the storage
  bellows

panpipe /'pan,piep, ,-'-/ *n*, **panpipes** *n taking sing or pl vb*
  a primitive wind instrument consisting of a graduated series
  of short vertical pipes bound together with the mouthpieces
  in an even row

Panufnik, Andrzej /,pa'noofnik/
  (born 1914) Polish conductor and composer

parlando[1] /par'lan,doh/ *adv or adj*

delivered or performed in an unsustained style or manner suggestive of speech

parlando² *n*

    1 parlando style – compare CANTABILE

    2 a piece or passage in parlando style

parlante /pah'lantay/ *adv or adj*

    parlando

parody¹ /'parədi/ *n*

    a literary or musical work in which the style of an author is imitated for comic or satirical effect – **parodic** *adj*, **parodist** *n*

parody² *vt*

    to compose a parody on

Parry, Sir (Charles) Hubert (Hastings) /'pari/

    (1848–1918) English composer; works include much choral music (e g *Ode on St Cecilia's Day* and *Blessed Pair of Sirens*) and songs (e g *Jerusalem*)

Parry, John

    'Blind Parry' (c1710–82) Welsh music collector and harpist

part /paht/ *n*

    1 a vocal or instrumental line or melody in concerted music or in harmony

    2 (the score for) a particular voice or instrument in concerted music

par terre /,pah 'teə/ *adv or adj*

    of a movement in ballet along the ground; on the floor – compare EN L'AIR

partial /'pahsh(ə)l/ *n*

    an overtone

partita /pah'teetə/ *n*

    a musical suite

partitur /,pahti'too(ə)/ , **partitura** /-'toorə/ *n*

    a full score showing each part on a separate line or staff

partner /'pahtnə/ *n*

either of a couple who dance together

part-song *n*

a usu unaccompanied song consisting of 2 or more voice parts with 1 part carrying the melody

pas /pah/ *n, pl* **pas** /~, pahz/

a dance step or combination of steps

pas de basque /ˌpa də 'bask, 'bahsk/ *n*

a dance step alternating from side to side in 3 counts that is characteristic of the Basque national dance

pas de bourrée /ˌpa də 'booray/ *n*

a sideways step in ballet in which one foot crosses behind or in front of the other

pas de deux /ˌpah də 'duh/ *n, pl* **pas de deux** /~, duhz/

a dance or set of dance steps for 2 performers

pas glissé /ˌpa 'gleesay, gli'say/ *n*

a gliding step in ballet

paso doble /ˌpasoh 'dohblay/ *n*

(the music for) a ballroom dance in time based on a Latin American march step and associated with bullfighting

passacaglia /ˌpasə'kahlyə/ *n*

1 an instrumental composition in moderately slow triple time consisting of variations usu on a ground bass

2 (a dance performed to) an old Italian or Spanish dance tune

passage /'pasij/ *n*

a phrase or short section of a composition

passamezzo , passemezzo /ˌpasə'metsoh/ *n*

(the music for) an old originally Italian dance in duple time resembling the pavane but about as twice as fast

passepied /pah'spyay/ *n*

a lively 17th- and 18th-c dance of French peasant origin, resembling the minuet and beginning on the last beat of the bar; *also* the music for this dance typically found in suites

passing note *n*

a melodic but discordant note interposed between essential
notes of adjacent chords

passion /'pash(ə)n/ *n*
a musical setting of a gospel account of the Passion story –
passional *adj*

passionato /ˌpasiə'nahtoh, -syə-, ˌpashə-/ *adv or adj*
in a passionate manner; with passion; fervently

pastiche /pa'steesh/ *n*
1 a literary, artistic, or musical work that imitates the style
of a previous work
2 a musical, literary, or artistic composition made up of
elements borrowed from various sources

pastoral /'pahst(ə)rəl/ *n*
a pastorale

pastorale /ˌpastə'rahli/ *n*
an instrumental composition or opera with a pastoral theme

patetico /pə'taytikoh/ *adv or adj*
with feeling; movingly

patter song *n*
a comic song marked by the rapid and well-articulated
delivery of a string of words accompanied by a simple tune

Patti, Adelina /'pati/
(1843–1919) Italian (Spanish-born) operatic soprano

Paul Jones /ˌpawl 'johnz/ *n*
a dance during which the couples change partners

pausa /'powza/ *n*
a rest or pause

pause /pawz/ *n*
the sign denoting a fermata – see illustration at DIRECTION

pavane *also* **pavan** /pə'van, pə'vahn, 'pavən/ *n*
(music for or having the slow duple rhythm of) a stately
court dance by couples that was introduced from South
Europe into England in the 16th c. It often preceded and
supplied the material for a galliard.

Pavarotti, Luciano /ˌpavəˈroti/
(born 1936) Italian tenor

Pavlova, Anna /ˈpavləvə, pavˈlohvə/
(1885–1931) Russian ballerina

peal /peel/ n
1 a complete set of changes on a given number of bells
2 a ring; *specif* one tuned to the notes of the major scale for
change ringing
3 the sound made when a set of bells is rung

Pears, Sir Peter /ˈpiəz/
(born 1910) English tenor

pedal /ˈpedl/ n
1 a lever pressed by the foot in playing a musical instrument
2 a pedal point

pedal board n
a pedal keyboard esp of a pipe organ

pedal-note n
1 a pedal point
2 any of the lowest notes that can be sounded on a brass
instrument being an octave below the normal usable range
and representing the fundamental of the harmonic series

pedal organ n
the portion of a pipe organ that is controlled from the pedal
keyboard

pedal point, pedal n
a single note, usu the tonic or dominant, that is normally
sustained in the bass and sounds against changing harmonies
in other parts

peg /peg/ n
any of the wooden pins set in the head of a stringed
instrument and turned to regulate the pitch of the strings

pegbox n
the open part of the head in a stringed instrument in which
the pegs are set

pellet /ˈpelit/ *n*
the small unattached ball within the body of certain bells by
which they are sounded

Penderecki, Krzysztof /ˌpendəˈretski/
(born 1933) Polish composer

penny whistle *n*
a tin whistle

pentatonic scale /ˌpentəˈtonik/ *n*
a scale consisting of 5 notes; *specif* one in which the notes
are arranged like a major scale with the fourth and seventh
notes omitted

Pepusch, Johann Christoph /peˈpoohsh/
(1667-1752) British (German-born) composer; arranged
music for *The Beggar's Opera*

percussion /pəˈkush(ə)n/ *n*
1 the beating or striking of an instrument
2 *taking sing or pl vb* percussion instruments that form a
section of a band or orchestra – **percussion** *adj*, **percussive**
adj

percussion instrument *n*
an instrument (e g a drum or xylophone) sounded by
striking, shaking, or scraping

percussionist /pəˈkush(ə)nist/ *n*
one who plays percussion instruments

perdendosi /puhˈdendoh,si/ *adv or adj*
dying away

perfect /ˈpuhfikt/ *adj*
1 *of the intervals fourth, fifth, and octave* having a character
that is retained when inverted; not augmented or
diminished – compare MAJOR, MINOR
2 *of a cadence* passing from a dominant or subdominant to a
tonic chord – **perfectness** *n*

perfect pitch *n*
ABSOLUTE PITCH 2

Pergolesi, Giovanni Battista /ˌpuhgə'layzi/
(1710–36) Italian composer, esp of operas, cantatas, and sacred music

périgourdine /periˌgooə'deen/ *n*
an old French dance in quick sextuple time the tune of which was sung by the dancers

pesante /pe'zantay/ *adv*
in a heavy manner

Peterson, Oscar (Emmanuel) /'peetəˌsən/
(born 1925) American jazz pianist

Philharmonic /ˌfilə'monik, ˌfil(h)ah-/ *n*
a symphony orchestra

Philidor, François André /'filidaw/
né *Danican* (1726–95) French chess player and composer; works include choral music and operas

phrase¹ /frayz/ *n*
a group of notes forming a natural unit of melody

phrase² *vt*
to divide into melodic phrases

phrasing /'frayzing/ *n*
the art, act, method, or result of grouping notes into phrases

phrygian mode /'friji·ən/ *n, often cap P*
an authentic mode which may be represented on the white keys of the piano on a scale from E to E

piacevole /pya'chayvohˌlay/ *adv or adj*
pleasantly, agreeably

Piaf, Edith /'pee,af/
née *Edith Giovanna Gassion* (1915–63) French cabaret singer

piangevole /pyan'jay,vohlay/ *adv or adj*
plaintively

pianissimo /ˌpee·ə'nisimoh/ *adv or adj*
very soft

pianist /'pee·ənist/ *n*
a skilled performer on the piano

pianistic /ˌpee·əˈnistik/ *adj*
1 of or characteristic of the piano
2 skilled in or well adapted to piano playing – **pianistically** *adv*

piano¹ /piˈahnoh, 'pyah-/ *adv or adj*
in a soft or quiet manner

piano² /piˈanoh/ *n, pl* **pianos**
a stringed instrument having steel wire strings that sound when struck by felt-covered hammers operated from a keyboard

pianoforte /ˌpyanohˈfawti, pi,ah-, pi,a-/ *n*
a piano

Pianola /ˌpee·əˈnohlə/ *trademark*
– used for a mechanical piano operated by the pressure of air through perforations in a paper roll

piano score *n*
a reduction of an orchestral score to a piano version

Piatigorsky, Gregor /ˌpee·atiˈgawski/
(1903–76) American (Russian-born) cellist

pibroch /'peebrok(h)/ *n*
a set of martial or mournful variations for the Scottish Highland bagpipe

piccolo /'pikəˌloh/ *n, pl* **piccolos**
1 a small shrill flute whose range is an octave higher than that of an ordinary flute
2 a 2-foot labial pipe-organ stop with a high piercing tone – **piccoloist** *n*

pick¹ /pik/ *vt*
to pluck with a plectrum or with the fingers <~ *a guitar*>

pick² *n*
a plectrum

pick out *vt*

to play the notes of by ear or one by one <*learned to* pick out *tunes on the piano*>

piece /pees/ *n*
a literary, artistic, dramatic, or musical work

pillar /ˈpilə/ *n*
the vertical hollow post of a harp frame

pin /pin/ *n*
a peg – **pinned** *adj*

Pinza, Ezio /ˈpinzə/
(1892–1957) Italian bass

pipe¹ /piep/ *n*
1 a tubular wind instrument; *specif* a small fipple flute held in and played with one hand, esp while a tabor is played with the other
2 a flue pipe
3 a reed pipe
4 **pipes** *pl*, **pipe** a bagpipe

pipe² *vb*
1 to play (a tune) on a pipe
2 to utter in the shrill tone of a pipe

pipe major *n*
the principal player in a band of bagpipes

pipe organ *n*
ORGAN 1

piper /ˈpiepə/ *n*
one who plays on a pipe

piping /ˈpieping/ *n*
the music of a pipe

pirouette /ˌpirooˈet/ *n*
a full turn made while balanced on the half point, quarter point, or full point of one leg – **pirouette** *vi*

piston /ˈpist(ə)n/ *n*
1 a sliding valve in a cylinder in a brass instrument that is used to lower its pitch

2 a button on an organ console for bringing in a preselected registration

pitch¹ /pich/ *vt*

to set in a particular pitch or key

pitch² *n*

1 the property of a sound, esp a note, that is determined by the frequency of the waves producing it; highness or lowness of sound

2 a standard frequency for tuning instruments – **pitched** *adj*

pitch pipe *n*

a small instrument of 1 or more reeds or fine pipes blown to establish the pitch in singing or in tuning an instrument

più /'pyooh, pi'ooh/ *adv*

more – used to qualify another adverb or adjective that is used as a direction

pizz. *adv or adj*

pizzicato

pizzicato /ˌpitsiˈkahtoh/ *n, adv, or adj, pl* **pizzicati** /-ti/

(a note or passage played) by means of plucking instead of bowing stringed instruments

plagal /'playgl/ *adj*

1 *of a church mode* having the keynote on the 4th scale step – compare AUTHENTIC

2 *of a cadence* passing from a subdominant to a tonic chord

plainchant /'playn,chahnt/ *n*

plainsong

plainsong /-,song/ *n*

1 the nonmetrical monophonic music of the medieval church; *esp* a Gregorian chant

2 a liturgical chant of any of various Christian rites

play /play/ *vb*

1 *vi* to perform music

2 *vi* to sound in performance <*the organ is* ~*ing*>

3 *vi* to reproduce or emit sounds <*his radio is* ~*ing*> ~

4 *vt* to perform (music) on an instrument <~ *a waltz*>

5 *vt* to perform music of (a specified composer) – **playable**
adj, **player** *n*, **playability** *n*

player piano /'pleɪə/ *n*
  a piano containing a mechanical device that operates the
  keys automatically

plectrum /'plektrəm/ *n*, *pl* **plectra** /-trə/, **plectrums**
  a small thin piece of plastic, metal, etc used to pluck the
  strings of a stringed instrument

plié /'plee·ay/ *n*
  the action in ballet of bending the knees outwards while
  holding the back straight

Plisetskaya, Maiya Mikhailovna /,pliset'skieyə/
  (born 1925) Soviet ballet dancer

pluck /pluk/ *vt*
  to play (an instrument) by picking or pulling at the strings –
  plucker *n*

plunk /plungk/ *vt*
  to pluck so as to produce a hollow, metallic, or harsh sound

pochetto /po'ketoh/, **pochettino** /,poke'teenoh/ *n*
  a very little

pochissimo /po'keesimoh/ *adv or adj*
  as small as possible

poco /'pohkoh/ *adv*
  slightly, somewhat <~ *allegro*>

poco a poco *adv*
  gradually

podium /'pohdi·əm/ *n*, *pl* **podiums, podia** /-di·ə/
  a small raised platform (for an orchestral conductor)

point /poynt/ *n*
  1 *usu pl* the tip of the toes – used in ballet
  2 the head of the bow of a stringed instrument

pointe /pwant/ *n*
  a ballet position in which the body is balanced on the

extreme tip of the toe

pointing /ˈpoynting/ n
a method used in Anglican chant to indicate which portion
of a verse is to be recited and which inflected

polacca /pohˈlakə/ n
a polonaise

polka /ˈpolkə/ n
(music for or in the rhythm of) a vivacious dance of
Bohemian origin in duple time and having a basic pattern of
hop-step-close-step – **polka** vi

polonaise /ˌpoləˈnayz/ n
(music in moderate time for) a stately Polish processional
dance popular in 19th-c Europe

polska /ˈpohlzkə, ˈpohlskə/ n
(the music, usu in a minor key, for) a Swedish folk dance
derived from a Polish peasant dance and in triple time

polyphonic /ˌpoliˈfonik/ , **polyphonous** /pəˈlifənəs/ adj
of or marked by polyphony – compare HOMOPHONIC –
polyphonically adv, **polyphonously** adv

polyphony /pəˈlifəni/ n
a style of composition in which 2 or more independent but
related voice parts sound against one another

polyrhythm /-ˌridh(ə)m/ n
the simultaneous combination of contrasting rhythms –
polyrhythmic adj, **polyrhythmically** adv

polytonality /-tohˈnaləti/ n
the simultaneous use of 2 or more keys – **polytonal** adj,
polytonally adv

Ponchielli, Amilcare /ˌpongkiˈeli/
(1834–86) Italian composer, esp of operas (e g La
Gioconda)

Pons, Lily /pohns/
(1904–76) American (French-born) soprano

ponticello /ˌpontiˈcheloh/ n

1 the bridge of a bowed stringed instrument

2 a change in register in the voice (e g of a boy at puberty); a break

pop¹ /pop/ *adj*

of pop music <~ *singer*>

pop² *n*

pop music

pop music *n*

modern commercially promoted popular music that is usu short and simple and has a strong beat

portamento /ˌpawtəˈmentoh/ *n, pl* **portamenti** /-ti/

a continuous gliding movement from one note to another by the voice, a trombone, or a bowed stringed instrument

port de bras /ˌpaw də ˈbrah/ *n*

the technique and practice of arm movement in ballet

Porter, Cole Albert /ˈpawtə/

(1891–1964) American composer and songwriter

position /pəˈzish(ə)n/ *n*

1 the disposition of the notes of a chord

2 a term used to denote the position of a string player's left hand on the fingerboard <*first* ~>

post horn *n*

a simple wind instrument with cupped mouthpiece used esp by postilions in the 18th and 19th c

Poulenc, Francis /ˈpooh,longk/

(1899–1963) French pianist and composer; works include many piano pieces, choral music, and songs

Powell, Maud /ˈpow(ə)l/

(1868–1920) American violinist

pp , *ppp* *adv or adj*

pianissimo

Praetorius, Michael /ˌprieˈtawri·əs/

(1571–1621) German composer and author; wrote *Syntagma Musicum*, a treatise on music and musical instruments of the

16th and 17th c

precentor /pri'sentə/ *n*
a leader of the singing of a choir or congregation –
precentorship *n*, **precentorial** *adj*

preces /'prayseez/ *n pl*
short petitions or prayers uttered by the priest and
responded to by the choir and/or congregation

precipitato /pri,sipi'tahtoh/ , **precipitoso** /-'tohsoh, -zoh/ *adv*
or adj
precipitately, impetuously

prelude /'prelyoohd/ *n*
1 a section or movement introducing the theme or chief
subject or serving as an introduction (e g to an opera)
2 a short separate concert piece, usu for piano or orchestra
– **preludial** *adj*

preside /pri'zied/ *vi*
to perform as featured or chief instrumentalist – usu + *at*
<~d *at the organ*> – **presider** *n*

Presley, Elvis Aaron /'prezli/
(1935–77) American pop singer

prestissimo /pre'stisi,moh/ *n, adv, or adj*
(a composition or movement to be played) at a very rapid
tempo

presto /'prestoh/ *n, adv, or adj, pl* **prestos**
(a passage or movement played) at a rapid tempo

Previn, André George /'previn/
(born 1929) American (German-born) conductor, pianist,
and composer

prima ballerina /'preemə/ *n*
the principal female dancer in a ballet company

prima donna /,preemə 'donə/ *n, pl* **prima donnas**
the principal female singer in an opera (company)

prima volta[1] /,preemə 'voltə/ *adv or adj*
at the first time – used as a direction to perform the first

time but omit at the repetition

prima volta², **prima** *n*

a part (to be) performed prima volta

primo /'preemoh/ *n, pl* **primos** /-mohz/

the first or leading part (e g in a duet or trio)

principal /'prinsipl/ *n*

1 the chief open metallic stop in an English pipe organ that is an octave above the open diapason and consists of a 4-foot stop on the manual and an 8-foot stop on the pedal

2 *often cap* an octave or 4-foot stop – usu in combination <*dulciana* Principal>

3 the chief motif or feature in a work of art

4 a fugue subject – compare ANSWER

prisiadka, **prisjadka** /pris'yadkə/ *n*

a Slavic male dance step executed by extending the legs alternately forward from a squatting position

Pritchard, Sir John Michael /'prichahd, -əd/

(born 1921) English conductor

processional /prə'sesh(ə)nl/ *n*

a composition (e g a hymn) designed for a procession

programmatic /ˌprohgrə'matik/ *adj*

of programme music – **programmatically** *adv*

programme music *n*

music intended to suggest a sequence of images or incidents

progression /prə'gresh(ə)n/ *n*

succession of notes or chords – **progressional** *adj*

Prokofiev, Sergei Sergeevich /prə'kofi·ef, -yev/

(1891–1953) Russian pianist and composer; works include operas (e g *The Love for Three Oranges*) and ballets (e g *Romeo and Juliet*), violin and piano concertos, symphonies, piano music, and the monologue with orchestral accompaniment, *Peter and the Wolf*

prom /prom/ *n*

a promenade concert

promenade /ˈpr[oə]ˌnahd, ˌ--'-/ *vb*
to walk (one's dancing partner) about

promenade concert *n*
a concert at which some of the audience stand or can walk about

promenader /pr[oə]ˈnahdə/ *n*
someone attending a promenade concert

proper /ˈpropə/ *n, often cap*
the parts of the Mass, *Introit, Gradual, Offertory*, and *Communion*, that vary according to the liturgical calendar and are not set for chorus – compare ORDINARY

prothalamion /ˌprohthəˈlaymi·ən/ , **prothalamium** /-mi·əm/ *n, pl* **prothalamia** /-mi·ə/
a song or poem in celebration of a forthcoming marriage

Prout, Ebenezer /prowt/
(1835–1909) English composer, organist, and author, esp of a series of theoretical works and textbooks

psalm /sahm/ *n often cap*
any of the sacred songs attributed to King David and collected in the Book of Psalms

psalmody /ˈsahmədi, ˈsalmədi/ *n*
(the practice or art of) singing psalms in worship

psaltery *also* **psaltry** /ˈsawlt(ə)ri/ *n*
an ancient stringed instrument similar to the dulcimer but plucked

Puccini, Giacomo /poohˈcheeni/
(1858–1924) Italian opera composer; works include *La Bohème, Tosca*, and *Madam Butterfly*

pullthrough /ˈpoolˌthrooh/ *n*
a weighted cord with a piece of cloth attached that is passed through a tube of a woodwind instrument to clean it

pulse /puls/ *n*
BEAT 1

punk rock *n*

a style of rock music characterized by a driving tempo,
crude or obscene lyrics, and an aggressive delivery

Purcell, Henry /ˌpuh'sel/
(1659–95) English composer and organist; works include
songs and cantatas, church music, stage music (e g *Dido and
Aeneas*), chamber music, and keyboard works

pure /pyooə/ *adj,*
of a musical sound being in tune and free from harshness –
pureness *n*

Q

quadrille /kwə'dril/ *n*
   (the music for) a square dance for 4 couples made up of 5 or
   6 figures

quadruple /'kwodroopl, kwo'droohpl/ *adj*
   marked by 4 beats per bar <~ *time*> – **quadruply** *adv*

quadruplet /'kwodrooplit, kwo'droohplit/ *n*
   a group of 4 notes performed in the time of 3 notes of the
   same value

quarter note *n*
   NAm a crotchet

quarter rest *n*
   NAm a rest of the same time value as a quarter note

quarter tone *n*
   1 an interval of half a semitone
   2 a note at an interval of 1 quarter tone

quartet *also* **quartette** /kwaw'tet/ *n*
   (a composition for) a group of 4 instruments, voices, or
   performers

quasi /'kwahzi/ *adv*
   in effect <*andante* ~ *allegro*>; approximately <~ *largo*> –
   used to qualify a direction

quaver[1] /'kwayvə/ *vb*
   to speak or sing in a trembling voice – **quaveringly** *adv*,
   quavery *adj*

quaver[2] *n*
   a note with the time value of half a crotchet – see
   illustration at NOTE

quaver rest *n*
   a rest of the same time value as a quaver

quickstep /'kwik,step/ *n*
   (a piece of music composed for) a fast fox-trot characterized

by a combination of short rapid steps

quill /'kwil/ *n*

a plectrum for plucking the strings of a harpsichord, lute, or similar instrument

Quilter, Roger /'kwiltə/

(1877–1953) English composer

quintet *also* **quintette** /kwin'tet/ *n*

(a composition for) a group of 5 instruments, voices, or performers

quintuplet /'kwintyooplit, kwin'tyoohplit/ *n*

a group of 5 equal notes performed in the time given to 3, 4, etc of the same value

quire /kwie·ə/ *n*

archaic a choir

R

Rachmaninoff, Sergei Wassilievitch /rak'mani,nof, -,nov/
(1873–1943) Russian pianist, conductor, and composer;
works include operas, 3 symphonies, 4 piano concertos,
songs and piano pieces

rag /rag/ *n*
(a composition or dance in) ragtime

raga /'rahgə/ *n*
(an improvisation based on) any of the ancient traditional
melodic patterns or modes in Indian music

ragtime /'rag,tiem/ *n*
(music, esp for the piano, having) rhythm characterized by
strong syncopation in the melody with a regularly accented
accompaniment

Rainey, Gertrude /'rayni/
'*Mother of the Blues*' (1886–1939) American blues singer

rall. *adj or adv*
rallentando

rallentando /,ralən'tandoh/ *n, adj, or adv, pl* **rallentandos,
rallentandi** /-di/
(a passage performed) with a gradual decrease in tempo

Rambert, Dame Marie /'rom,beə/
née *Cynthia Rabbam* (1888–1982) British (Polish-born)
ballet dancer, teacher, and choreographer

Rameau, Jean Philippe /ra'moh/
(1683–1764) French music theorist and composer, esp of
ballets and operas; published several scientific-musical
treatises

range /raynj/ *n*
the extent of pitch within a melody or within the capacity of
a voice or instrument

rank /'rangk/ *n*

a series or set of organ pipes of the same construction and
quality having one pipe for each key

rasch /rash/ *adv or adj*
quick

rataplan /ˌratəˈplan, ˈ--ˌ-/ *n*
the sound of drumming

rattle[1] /ˈratl/ *vb*
to (cause to) make a series of short sharp sounds

rattle[2] *n*
1 a rattling sound
2 a device that produces a rattle; *esp* a device that consists
of a springy tongue in contact with a revolving ratchet wheel
that is rotated or shaken to produce a loud noise and is used
as a percussion instrument

Ravel, Maurice Joseph /rəˈvel/
(1875–1937) French composer; works include many piano
pieces, songs, a ballet, and the orchestral piece, *Bolero*

Rawsthorne, Alan /ˈrawsˌthawn/
(1905–71) English composer

ray, re /ray, ree/ *n*
the 2nd note of the diatonic scale in solmization

reading /ˈreeding/ *n*
a particular performance of something (e g a musical work)

real·ize, -ise /ˈreeliez, ˈriə-/ *vt*
to play or write (music) in full (e g from a figured bass) –
realizable *adj*, **realization** *n*

rebec, rebeck /ˈreebek/ *n*
a medieval pear-shaped usu 3-stringed instrument played
with a bow

recapitulation /ˌreekəpityooˈlaysh(ə)n/ *n*
the last of 3 parts of a movement written in sonata form in
which the main theme is repeated with modifications –
compare DEVELOPMENT, EXPOSITION

recessional /riˈsesh(ə)nl/ *n*

a hymn or musical piece at the conclusion of a church service

recital /ri'sietl/ *n*
a concert or public performance given by a musician, small group of musicians, or dancer – **recitalist** *n*

recitation /ˌresi'taysh(ə)n/ *n*
the section of a verse in Gregorian chant or plainsong that is sung on the reciting note or monotone

recitative /ˌresitə'teev/ *n*
(a passage delivered in) a style for singing a narrative text in which the rhythms and variations in pitch of the speaking voice are imitated – **recitative** *adj*

reciting note *n*
a note on which a varying number of syllables are uttered in chanting as distinguished from a note that receives but one syllable

recorder /ri'kawdə/ *n*
any of a group of wind instruments consisting of a slightly tapering tube with usu 8 finger holes and a mouthpiece like a whistle

redowa /'redəwə, -dəvə/ *n*
either of 2 popular Bohemian ballroom dances of the 19th c:
a a dance in triple time resembling a waltz
b a dance in time resembling a polka

reed /reed/ *n*
1 a thin elastic tongue or flattened tube (e g of cane or plastic) fastened over an air opening in an instrument (e g an organ or clarinet) and set in vibration by an air current
2 a woodwind instrument having a reed <*the* ~s *of an orchestra*>

reed organ *n*
a keyboard wind instrument in which the wind acts on a set of reeds

reed pipe *n*

an organ pipe producing its tone by vibration of a beating
reed in an air current

reed stop *n*
a set of reed pipes in a pipe organ controlled by a single
stop knob and constructed to be generally imitative of some
orchestral instrument

reel /reel, riəl/ *n*
(the music in ⁴ or ⁴ time for) a lively esp Scottish-Highland
or Irish dance in which 2 or more couples perform a series
of circular figures and winding movements

Reeves, Jim /reevz/
(1924–64) American singer

refrain /ri'frayn/ *n*
(the musical setting of) a regularly recurring phrase or
verse, esp at the end of each stanza or division of a poem or
song; a chorus

regal /'reegl/ *n*
a small portable organ used from the 15th to the 17th c

Reger, Max /'raygə/
(1873–1916) German composer

reggae /'regay/ *n*
popular music of West Indian origin that is characterized by
a strongly accented subsidiary beat

regisseur, régisseur /,rayzhi'suh/ *n*
a director responsible for staging a theatrical work (e g a
ballet)

register /'rejistə/ *n*
1 an organ stop
2 (a part of) the range of a human voice or a musical
instrument

rejdovàčka /raydoh'vahchkə/ , **rejdovák** /-'vahk/ *n*
a Bohemian dance in duple time, somewhat resembling the
polka but considered to be a variant of the redowa

related /ri'laytid/ *adj*

of notes, chords, or tonalities having close harmonic
connection – **relatedly** *adv*, **relatedness** *n*
relative /'relətiv/ *adj*,
of major and minor keys and scales having the same key
signature – **relatively** *adv*, **relativeness** *n*
repeat /ri'peet/ *n*
(a sign placed before or after) a passage to be repeated in
performance – see illustration at DIRECTION
repertoire /'repə,twah/, **repertory** /-,t(ə)ri/ *n*
a list or supply of dramas, operas, pieces, or parts that a
company or person is prepared to perform
répétiteur /ri,peti'tuh/ *n*
someone who coaches opera singers
repetizone /repeti'zohnay/, **repetizione** /repetitsi'ohnay/ *n*
repetition
replica /'rayplikə/ *n*
repetition
reprise /ri'preez/ *n*
a repetition of a passage, theme, or performance
requiem /'rekwi·əm, -,em/ *n, often cap*
1 a musical setting of the mass for the dead. The main parts
include the introit, *Requiem aeternam,* the *Kyrie, Dies Irae,
Sanctus,* and *Agnus Dei.*
2 a composition in honour of the dead
reservoir /'rezə,vwah/ *n*
a chamber in a pipe organ in which the compressed air
supplied by the blower is kept at a uniform pressure
resolution /,rezə'loohsh(ə)n, -'lyoohsh(ə)n/ *n*
the passing of a voice part from a dissonant to a consonant
note or the progression of a chord from dissonance to
consonance
resolve /ri'zolv/ *vb*
1 *vt* to make (e g voice parts) progress from dissonance to
consonance

2 *vi* to progress from dissonance to consonance – **resolvable**
adj, **resolver** *n*

resonance /ˈrezənəns/ *n*
the intensification and enrichment of a note by
supplementary vibration

resonator /ˈrezənaytə/ *n*
something that resounds or resonates; *specif* a device that
responds to and can be used to detect a particular frequency

Respighi, Ottorino /resˈpigi/
(1879–1936) Italian composer; works include operas,
chamber music, and some orchestral pieces

response /riˈspons/ *n*
a reply made by the choir and/or congregation to the preces
or versicles of the priest

rest /rest/ *n*
(a character representing) a silence of a specified duration –
see illustration at NOTE

retardation /ˌreetahˈdaysh(ə)n/ *n*
a suspension in which the suspended note is resolved
upwards instead of downwards

reverb /riˈvuhb, ˈree,vuhb/ *n*
(a usu electronic device for producing) an artificial echo
effect in recorded music

rf adv or adj
rinforzando

rhapsody /ˈrapsədi/ *n*
a composition of irregular form suggesting improvisation –
rhapsodic, rhapsodical *adj*, **rhapsodically** *adv*

rhumba /ˈrumbə/ *n*
a rumba

rhythm /ˈridh(ə)m/ *n*
1 (the aspect of music concerning) the regular recurrence of
a pattern of stress and length of notes
2 a characteristic rhythmic pattern <*music in rumba* ∼>;

also metre

3 rhythm, rhythm section *taking sing or pl vb* the group of instruments in a band (e g the drums, piano, and bass) supplying the rhythm

rhythm and blues *n*

popular music with elements of blues and Negro folk music

rib /'rib/ *n*

a curved side connecting the top and back of an instrument of the violin class

ricercare /,reecho'kahray/ , **ricercar** /'reechokah/ *n, pl* **ricercari** /-ri/, **ricercars**

any of various forms of usu contrapuntal instrumental music esp of the 16th and 17th c

rich /rich/ *adj*

full and mellow in tone and quality <*a ~ voice*> – **richness** *n*

Richard, Cliff /'richod/

pseudonym of *Harold Webb* (born 1940) English pop singer

Richter, Hans /'rik(h)to/

(1843–1916) Austrian (Hungarian-born) conductor

Richter, Sviatoslav

(born 1915) Soviet pianist

riff /rif/ *n*

(a piece based on) a constantly repeated phrase in jazz or rock music, typically played as a background to a solo improvisation – **riff** *vi*

rigadoon /,rigo'doohn/ *n*

a rigaudon

rigaudon /righo'donh/ *n*

(music in duple time for) a lively French dance of the 17th and 18th c

rigoroso /rigaw'rohsoh, -zoh/ *adv or adj*

strictly

Rimsky-Korsakov, Nikolai Andreevich

/ˌrim(p)ski'kawsəˌkof, -ˌkov/
(1844–1908) Russian composer; works include 15 operas, 3 symphonies, the symphonic suite *Sheherazade*, choral music, and songs

rinforzando /ˌrinfaw'tsandoh/ *adv or adj*
played with an increase of force; reinforcing – used as a direction for special emphasis of a note, chord, or short phrase; compare SFORZANDO

ring *n*
1 a set of bells
2 a clear resonant sound made by vibrating metal; *also* a similar sound
3 resonant tone
4 an act or instance of ringing

ringing /'ringing/ *n*
a vigorous method of sounding church bells in which the bell is swung round full circle – compare CHIMING

ripieno /ri'pyenoh/ *n, pl* **ripieni** /-ni/, **ripienos**
a supplementary or accompanying group of instruments or musical parts; *esp* all the instruments or musical parts except the soloist (e g in a concerto grosso)

risoluto /ˌrisə'loohtoh, ˌrizə-/ *adv or adj*
resolutely and with marked accent

risvegliato /ˌrisvayli'ahtoh, ˌriz-/ *adv or adj*
with increased animation

rit. *adv or adj*
ritenuto

ritard. *adv or adj*
ritardando

ritardando /ˌritah'dandoh/ *adv, adj, or n, pl* **ritardandos**
(with) a gradual slackening in tempo

ritenuto /ˌreete'n(y)oohtoh, ˌritə'nyoohtoh/ *adv, adj, or n, pl* **ritenutos**
(with) an immediate slackening of tempo

ritmico /'reetmikoh/ *adv or adj*
rhythmically

ritornello /ˌritaw'neloh/ *n, pl* **ritornelli** /-li/, **ritornellos**
1 a short recurrent instrumental passage in a vocal composition
2 a tutti passage in a concerto or rondo refrain

Robbins, Jerome /'robinz/
(born 1918) American dancer and choreographer

Robeson, Paul Bustill /'rohbsən/
(1898–1976) American actor and singer

Robinson, Stanford /'robinsən/
(1904–84) English conductor and composer

rock /rok/ , **rock and roll, rock 'n' roll** /ˌrok (ə)n 'rohl/ *n*
popular music, usu played on electronically amplified instruments and characterized by a persistent heavily accented beat, much repetition of simple phrases, and often country, folk, and blues elements

rococo¹ /ro'kohkoh, rə-/ *adj*
of an 18th-c musical style marked by light gay ornamentation

rococo² *n*
rococo work or style

Rodgers, Richard /'rojəz/
(1902–79) American composer, esp of musicals

Rodrigo, Joaquín /rod'reegoh/
(born 1902) Spanish composer; works include guitar concerto

Rogers, Ginger /'rojəz/
née *Virginia McMath* (born 1911) American actress and dancer

rohrflöte /'rohrˌfluhtə/ , **rohr flute** *n*
a pipe-organ flute stop having closed metal pipes with chimneys

roll¹ /rohl/ *vb*

1 *vt* to make a continuous beating sound on; sound a roll on
<~ed *their drums*>

2 *vt* to play (a chord) in arpeggio style

3 *vi* to make a deep reverberating sound

roll² *n*

1 a sound produced by rapid strokes on a drum

2 a chord in arpeggio style

romance /roh'mans, rə-/ *n*

a short lyrical piece

romanesca /ˌrohmə'neskə/ , **romanesque** /-'nesk/ *n*

a galliard

romantic /rə'mantik, roh-/ *adj*

of or being (a composer of) 19th-c music characterized by
an emphasis on subjective emotional qualities and freedom
of form – **romantically** *adv*

Romantic *n*

a romantic writer, artist, or composer

Romberg, Sigmund /'romˌbuhg/

(1887–1951) Hungarian-born composer, esp of operettas
(e g *The Student Prince*)

rond de jambe /ˌronh də 'zhahm/ *n, pl* **ronds de jambe**
/ˌronh(z)/

a circular movement of the leg in ballet either par terre or
en l'air

rondeña /ron'daynyə/ *n*

a fandango of southern Spain

rondo /'rondoh/ *n, pl* **rondos**

an instrumental composition, esp a movement in a concerto
or sonata, typically having a principal theme that alternates
with episodes on the plan A B A C A, where A is the
principal theme, and B and C the episodes

root /rooht/ *n*

the note from whose overtones a chord is composed; the
lowest note of a chord in normal position

rosin¹ /'rozin/ *n*
a translucent resin that is the residue from the distillation of turpentine and is used for rubbing on violin bows

rosin² *vt*
to rub or treat (the bow of a violin) with rosin

Rossini, Gioacchino Antonio /ro'sini/
(1792–1868) Italian composer; works include operas (e g *William Tell* and *The Barber of Seville*) and choral music

Rostropovich, Mstislav Leopoldovich /,rostrə'poh,vich/
(born 1927) Soviet cellist

roulade /,rooh'lahd/ *n*
an elaborate vocal embellishment sung to 1 syllable

round /rownd/ *n*
a usu unaccompanied canon sung in unison in which each part is continuously repeated

round dance *n*
1 a folk dance in which participants form a ring
2 a ballroom dance in which couples progress round the room

roundelay /'rowndi,lay/ *n*
a simple song with a refrain

Rozhdestvensky, Gennady /,rozhdest'venski/
(born 1931) Soviet conductor

rubato /rooh'bahtoh/ *n, pl* **rubatos**
expressive fluctuation of speed within a phrase

Rubbra, Edmund /'roohbrə/
(born 1901) English composer; works include symphonies, concertos for violin, viola, and piano, chamber music, the *Festival Overture*, and much choral music

Rubinstein, Anton /'roohbin,stien/
(1829–94) Russian pianist and composer

Rubinstein, Arthur
(1888–1983) American (Polish-born) pianist

Ruckers /'roohkuhs/

Flemish family of harpsichord makers thought to have made the earliest harpsichords with 2 manuals and a regular 4-foot stop

rueda /rooh'aydə/ *n*
a Spanish round dance in quintuple time

ruhig /'rooh·ikh/ *adv or adj*
in a calm and peaceful manner

rumba , rhumba /'rumbə/ *n*
(the music in $\frac{2}{4}$ or $\frac{4}{4}$ time for) a ballroom dance of Cuban Negro origin marked by steps with a delayed transfer of weight and pronounced hip movements

run¹ /run/ *vi*
to sing or play quickly <~ *up the scale*>

run² *n*
1 a rapid passage up or down a scale
2 a number of rapid small dance steps executed in even tempo – **runless** *adj*

S

Sachs, Hans /zaks, saks/
(1494–1576) German poet and Mastersinger

sackbut /'sak‚but/ *n*
a renaissance trombone

Saint-Léon, Arthur /‚sanh'layonh/
(1821–70) French ballet dancer and choreographer

Saint-Saëns, (Charles) Camille /'sanh‚sonh/
(1835–1921) French pianist and composer; works include
symphonic poems (e g *Danse Macabre*), symphonies, the
opera *Samson and Delilah*, and the zoological fantasy
Carnival of the Animals for 2 pianos and chamber ensemble

Salieri, Antonio /‚sali'eəri/
(1750–1825) Italian conductor, teacher, and composer of
operas and other works; the story of his poisoning Mozart
has no foundation

saltarello /‚saltə'reloh/ *n, pl* **salterellos**
an Italian dance with a lively hop step beginning each
measure

samba /'sambə/ *n*
(the music for) a Brazilian dance of African origin
characterized by a dip and spring upwards at each beat of
the music – **samba** *vi*

samisen /'sami‚sen/ *n*
a 3-stringed Japanese instrument resembling a banjo

saraband, sarabande /'sarəband, ‚--'-/ *n*
(a composition or movement in slow triple time with the
accent on the second beat for) a stately court dance
resembling the minuet, one of the movements of a suite

sardana /sar'donə/ *n*
(the music, usu in time and played on the fife and tabor,
for) a Catalan dance in which participants form a ring and

move alternately to the left and right with long and short
steps

Sargent, Sir (Harold) Malcolm (Watts) /'sahjənt/
(1895–1967) English conductor

sarod /sə'rohd/ n
a lute of North India – **sarodist** n

sarrusophone /sə'roohzəfohn, -'ru-/ n
a double-reed woodwind instrument of the oboe family that
is made of metal and is used esp in military bands

Satie, Erik Alfred Leslie /'sahti/
(1866–1925) French composer; works include piano music,
songs, and ballets

sax /saks/ n
a saxophone

Sax, (Antoine Joseph) Adolphe /saks/
(1814–94) Belgian musician; inventor of the saxophone and
saxhorn

saxhorn /'saks,hawn/ n
any of a group of valved brass instruments with a conical
tube, oval shape, and cup-shaped mouthpiece

saxophone /'saksə,fohn/ n
any of a group of single-reed woodwind instruments having
a conical metal tube and finger keys and used esp in jazz
and popular music – **saxophonist** n

scale /skayl/ n
a graduated series of notes ascending or descending in order
of pitch according to a specified scheme of their intervals –
scalic adj

Scarlatti, Alessandro /,skah'lati/
father of Domenico, (1660–1725) Italian composer, esp of
opera and chamber cantatas

Scarlatti, (Giuseppe) Domenico
(1685–1757) Italian harpsichordist, pianist, and composer,
esp of keyboard and church music

scat /skat/ *n*
jazz singing with nonsense syllables – **scat** *vi*

scherzando /skeət'sandoh/ *n, adv, or adj, pl* **scherzandos**
(a passage or movement played) in a sprightly or playful
manner

scherzo /'skeətsoh/ *n, pl* **scherzos, scherzi** /-tsi/
a lively instrumental composition or movement in quick usu
triple time

scherzoso /ˌskeət'sohsoh, -zoh/ *adv or adj*
scherzando

Schnabel, Artur /'shnahb(ə)l/
(1882–1951) American (Austrian-born) pianist and
composer

schnell /'shnel/ *adv or adj*
fast

Schoenberg, Arnold /'shuhnˌbuhg/
(1874–1951) Austrian composer; works include
choral-orchestral music (e g *Gurrelieder*), chamber music,
and much atonal and twelve-note music

schottische /sho'teesh/ *n*
(music for) a round dance in duple time resembling a slow
polka

Schubert, Franz (Peter) /'shoohˌbuht/
(1797–1828) Austrian composer; works include over 600
songs, choral and chamber music, and orchestral pieces (e g
the *Unfinished Symphony*)

Schuman, William Howard /'shoohmən/
(born 1910) American composer

Schumann, Clara (Josephine) /'shoohˌman, -ˌmən/
née *Wieck*; wife of Robert, (1819–96) German pianist and
composer, esp of piano music

Schumann, Elisabeth
(1888–1952) American (German-born) soprano

Schumann, Robert (Alexander)

(1810–56) German composer; works include much piano and chamber music, 4 symphonies, a piano concerto, and many songs

Schütz, Heinrich /shoohts/
(1585–1672) German composer, esp of choral music

Schwarz, Rudolf /shwawts/
(born 1905) English (Austrian-born) conductor

Schwarzkopf, Elisabeth /'shvahts,kopf/
(born 1915) German soprano

Schweitzer, Albert /'s(h)wietsə, 'shvie-/
(1875–1965) French philosopher, theologian, physician, organist, and music scholar

scordatura /,skawdah'toohrah/ n
a 'mis-tuning' of stringed instruments to create special effects

score¹ /skaw/ n
1 the copy of a composition in written or printed notation
2 the music for a film or theatrical production
3 a complete description of a dance composition in choreographic notation

score² vt
1 to write or arrange (music) for specific voice or instrumental parts
2 to orchestrate
3 to compose a score for (e g a film) – **scorer** n

Scotto, Renata /'skotoh/
(born 1934) Italian soprano

Scriabin, Alexander /skri'ahbin/
(1872–1915) Russian pianist and composer; works include piano music and orchestral pieces (e g *Poem of Ecstasy*)

scroll /'skrohl/ n
the curved head of a bowed stringed instrument

Searle, Humphrey /suhl/
(1915–82) English composer

sec /sek/ *adv or adj*

　　detached

second¹ /'sekənd/ *adj or n*

　　(relating to or having) a part typically subordinate to or
　　lower in pitch than the first part in concerted or ensemble
　　music – **second, secondly** *adv*

second² *n*

　　1 (the harmonic combination of 2 notes at) an interval of 2
　　diatonic degrees

　　2 a note separated from another by this interval; *specif* the
　　supertonic

secondo /se'kondoh/ *n, pl* **secondi** /-di/

　　the second, usu lower, part in a concerted piece or duet

section /'seksh(ə)n/ *n*

　　a section of an orchestra composed of 1 class of instruments
　　(e g strings)

secular /'sekyoolə/ *adj*

　　not religious – **secularly** *adv*, **secularity** *n*

Seeger, Peter /'seegə/

　　'*Pete*' (born 1919) American folksinger

segno /'senyoh/ *n, pl* **segnos**

　　the sign that marks the beginning or end of a musical repeat
　　– see illustration at DIRECTION

Segovia, Andrés /se'gohvi·ə, -vyə/

　　(born 1893) Spanish guitarist and composer

segue¹ /'say,gwə, 'se-/ *vb imperative*

　　1 perform the music that follows at once – compare
　　ATTACCA

　　2 perform the music that follows like that which has
　　preceded

segue² *n*

　　a transition from one number to another – **segue** *vb*

seguidilla /,segi'dilyə, -'deel-/ *n*

　　a Spanish dance in triple time

sehr /zeə/ *adv*
very

semibreve /'semi,breev/ *n*
a note with the time value of 2 minims or 4 crotchets – see illustration at NOTE

semibreve rest *n*
a rest of the same time value as a semibreve

semiquaver /'semi,kwayvə/ *n*
a note with the time value of half a quaver – see illustration at NOTE

semiquaver rest *n*
a rest of the same time value as a semiquaver

semitone /'semi,tohn/ *n*
the interval of half a tone (e g E–F or F–F #) equal to the interval between 2 adjacent keys on a keyboard instrument – **semitonic** *adj*

semplice /'sempli,chay/ *adv or adj*
in a simple and unaffected manner

sempre /'sempri; *also* 'sempray/ *adv*
always <~ *legato*>

senza /'sentsah/ *prep*
without <~ *sordino*>

septet /sep'tet/ *n*
1 a composition for 7 instruments, voices, or performers
2 *taking sing or pl vb* a group of 7 performers

sequence /'seekwəns/ *n*
1 a succession of repetitions of a melodic phrase or harmonic pattern each in a new position – compare IMITATION
2 a hymn-like composition

serenade¹ /,serə'nayd/ *n*
originally a piece of music played out of doors in the evening; now a term for an instrumental composition in several movements written for a small ensemble

serenade² *vb*

to perform a serenade (in honour of) – **serenader** *n*

serial /'siəri·əl/ *adj*

of or being music based on a series of notes in an arbitrary but fixed order without regard for traditional tonality <~ *music*> <~ *technique*> – **serially** *adv*

serialism /'siəri·ə,liz(ə)m/ *n*

(the theory or practice of composing) serial music

Serkin, Rudolf /'suhkin/

(born 1903) American (Austrian-born) pianist

serpent /'suhpənt/ *n*

an old-fashioned bass woodwind instrument of serpentine form

service /'suhvis/ *n*

a musical setting of the canticles for *Morning Prayer* or *Evening Prayer*, or of the *Communion Service* in the Anglican church

Sessions, Roger /'seshənz/

(born 1896) American composer

set¹ /set/ *vb*

1 *vt* to provide music or instrumentation for (a text)

2 *vi* to dance face to face with another in a square dance <~ *to your partner*>

set² *n*

1 the basic formation in a country dance or square dance

2 (the music played at) a session of music (e g jazz or rock music), usu followed by an intermission

setting /'seting/ *n*

the music composed for a text (e g a poem)

seventh /'sev(ə)nth/ *n*

1 (the harmonic combination of 2 notes at) an interval of 7 diatonic degrees

2 a note separated by this interval from a root; *specif* the leading note – **seventh** *adj or adv*

seventh chord *n*
> a chord comprising a fundamental note with its third, fifth, and seventh

sevillana /ˌsevee(l)'yahnə/ *n*
> a seguidilla; *esp* the seguidilla as danced or played in Seville

sextet /sek'stet/ *n*
> **1** a composition for a group of 6 instruments, voices, or performers
> **2** a group of 6 performers

sextuple /ˌseks'tyoopl/ *adj*
> having 6 beats in a bar

sextuplet /'sekstyooplit/ *n*
> a group of 6 equal notes performed in the time ordinarily given to 4 or 5 of the same value

sf , *sfz* *adv or adj*
> sforzando

sforzando¹ /sfawt'sandoh/ *adj or adv*
> played with prominent stress or accent – used as a direction to indicate that a single note or chord is to be emphasized

sforzando² *n, pl* **sforzandos, sforzandi** /-di/
> an accented note or chord

sforzato /sfaw'tsahtoh/ *adv or adj*
> sforzando

shake /shayk/ *n*
> a trill – see illustration at DIRECTION

Shalyapin
> – see CHALIAPIN

Shankar, Ravi /'shang,kah/
> (born 1920) Indian musician

shanty, chanty /'shanti/ *n*
> a song sung by sailors in rhythm with their work

sharp¹ /shahp/ *adj*
> **1** *of a note* raised a semitone in pitch
> **2** higher than the intended pitch – **sharply** *adv*, **sharpness** *n*

**sharp² ** *adv*

above the proper pitch <*they're playing* ~>

**sharp³ ** *n*

1 a note 1 semitone higher than another indicated or previously specified note

2 a symbol on the staff indicating a raising in pitch of a semitone – see illustration at MUSIC

Sharp, Cecil (James) /shahp/

(1859–1924) English musician; responsible for the collection, publication, and performance of much English folk song and dance music; founded the *English Folk Dance and Song Society*

sharpen /'shahpən/ *vb*

to make or become sharp or sharper

shawm /shawm/ *n*

an early double-reed woodwind instrument

sheet music *n*

music printed on large unbound sheets of paper

shell /shel/ *n*

the hemispherical body of a kettledrum

shimmy¹ /'shimi/ *n*

a jazz dance characterized by a shaking of the body from the shoulders downwards

shimmy² *vi*

to shake, quiver, or tremble (as if) in dancing a shimmy

short score *n*

a reduction of a full orchestral or choral score to 2 staves

Shostakovich, Dmitri Dmitrievich /ˌshoshtəˈkoh,vich/

(1906–75) Soviet composer; works include 15 symphonies, string quartets, operas, violin, cello, and piano concertos, and much piano music

shoulder /'shohldə/ *n*

the rounded or sloping part of a stringed instrument (e g a double bass) where the neck joins the body – **shouldered** *adj*

shuffle¹ /'shufl/ *vi*
to dance in a lazy nonchalant manner with scraping and
tapping motions of the feet – **shuffler** *n*

shuffle² *n*
(a dance characterized by) a dragging sliding movement

shutter /'shutə/ *n*
the movable slots in the box enclosing the swell organ part
of a pipe organ, which are opened to increase the volume of
the sound – **shutterless** *adj*

si /see/ *n*
te – used in French and Italian fixed-doh solmization to
refer not to the 7th note of any scale, but to the note B in
whatever scale or context it may occur

Sibelius, Johan Julian Christian /si'bayli·əs, -lyəs/
(1865–1957) Finnish composer; works include much
nationalistic music such as the tone poem *Finlandia* and the
Legends (e g *The Swan of Tuonela*) as well as symphonies, a
violin concerto, and songs

siciliana /sə,sili'ahnə, sə,chi-/, **siciliano** /-'ahnoh/ *n*
(the music in $\frac{6}{8}$ or $\frac{12}{8}$ time for) a graceful rustic dance in
which the partners are joined with handkerchiefs

side drum *n*
a snare drum

sideman /'sied,man/ *n*
a member of a band or orchestra, esp a jazz or swing
orchestra, other than the leader or featured performer

siffleur /si'fluh, 'siflə/ *n*
one who whistles, esp as a musical performer

sight-read /'siet,reed/ *vb*
to read or perform (music) without previous preparation or
study – **sight-reader** *n*

sign /sien/ *n*
a symbol (e g a flat or sharp) used in musical notation

Silbermann, Gottfried /'silbə,man/

(1683–1753) German organ builder and piano and
clavichord maker

silvery /'silv(ə)ri/ *adj*

having a soft clear musical tone – **silveriness** *n*

Silvester, Victor (Marlborough) /sil'vestə/

(1900–78) English dance band leader

simile /'simi,lay/ *adv or adj*

similar – used as a direction to continue the same phrasing,
use of pedals, or whatever has been previously directed

simple time *n*

a metre (e g $\frac{2}{4}$) in which the main beats are divisible by 2 –
see illustration at TIME SIGNATURE

Sinatra, Francis Albert /si'nahtrə/

'*Frank*' (born 1915) American singer and film actor

sinfonia /,sinfə'nee·ə/ *n, pl* **sinfonie** /-'nee,ay/, **sinfonias**
SYMPHONY 1

sinfonietta /,sin,fohni'etə/ *n*

1 a short or lightly-orchestrated symphony
2 a small symphony orchestra; *also* a small orchestra of
strings only

sing /sing/ *vb*

1 *vi* to produce musical sounds by means of the voice
2 *vi* to utter words in notes and with musical inflections and
modulations (e g as a trained or professional singer)
3 *vi* to produce musical or melodious sounds
4 *vt* to utter with musical inflections; *esp* to interpret in
notes produced by the voice – **singable** *adj*, **singer** *n*

single reed *n*

a thin flat cane reed attached to the mouthpiece of certain
kinds of woodwind instrument

singsong /'sing,song/ *n*,
Br a session of group singing

Singspiel /'zing,shpee·əl/ *n*

a type of German opera with spoken dialogue

sistrum /'sistrəm/ *n, pl* **sistrums, sistra** /'sistrə/
an ancient percussion instrument, used esp in Egypt, with metal rods or loops that jingle when shaken

sitar /si'tah/ *n*
an Indian lute with a long neck and a varying number of strings – **sitarist** *n*

sixteen-foot stop, 16-foot stop *n*
a pipe-organ stop sounding pitches an octave lower than the notes indicate – compare EIGHT-FOOT STOP

sixteenth note /siks'teenth/ *n*
NAm a semiquaver

sixteenth rest *n*
NAm a rest of the same time value as a sixteenth note

sixth /siksth/ *n*
1 (the harmonic combination of 2 notes at) an interval of 6 diatonic degrees
2 a note at this interval; *specif* the submediant – **sixth** *adj*

sixth chord *n*
a chord consisting of a note with its third and its sixth, usu being the first inversion of a triad

sixty-fourth note *n*
NAm a hemidemisemiquaver

sixty-fourth rest *n*
NAm a rest of the same time value as a sixty-fourth note

ska /skah/ *n*
popular music of West Indian origin that is the forerunner of and similar to reggae

Skalkottas, Nikos /ˌskal'kotəs/
(1904–49) Greek composer

sketch /skech/ *n*
1 a short composition
2 a draft of a musical work or a jotting

skiffle /'skifl/ *n*
jazz or folk music played by a group and using nonstandard

instruments or noisemakers (e g washboards or Jew's harps)

skin /skin/ *n*

the membrane covering the head of a drum

skirl /skuhl/ *vi or n*

(to emit) the high shrill sound of a bagpipe

Skryabin

– see SCRIABIN

slargando /slah'gan,doh/ *adv or adj*

gradually slower; allargando

sleeve /sleev/ *n*

a paper or often highly distinctive cardboard covering that
protects a gramophone record when not in use

sleigh bell *n*

any of various bells similar to those attached to (the harness
of a horse drawing) a sleigh and used as percussion
instruments

slentando /slen'tandoh/ *adv or adj*

gradually decreasing in tempo

slide /slied/ *n*

1 a portamento

2 a U-shaped section of tube in the trombone that is pushed
out and in to produce notes of different pitch

3 an embellishment

slur¹ /sluh/ *vt*

to perform (successive notes of different pitch) in a smooth
or connected manner

slur² *n*

(a curved line connecting) notes to be sung to the same
syllable or performed without a break – see illustration at
MUSIC

Smetana, Bedřich /'smet(ə)nə/

(1824–84) Czech composer, pianist, and conductor; works
include operas (e g *The Bartered Bride*), symphonic poems,
and choral and piano music

Smith, Bessie /smith/
(1894–1937) American blues singer

Smith, John Stafford
(1750–1836) English organist and composer of part-songs, glees, catches, and anthems

smorz. *adv or adj*
smorzando

smorzando /smawt'sandoh/ *also* **smorzato** /-'sahtoh/ *adv or adj*
growing slower and softer; dying away

Smyth, Dame Ethel /smiedh/
(1858–1944) English author and composer, esp of operas

snare /sneə/ *n*
any of the catgut strings or metal spirals of a snare drum which produce a rattling sound

snare drum *n*
a small double-headed drum with 1 or more snares stretched across its lower head

soave /soh'ahvay/ *adv or adj*
with sweetness or smoothness; in a gentle manner –
soavemente *adv*

soft pedal *n*
a foot pedal on a piano that reduces the volume of sound by shortening the stroke of the hammers or by shifting the hammers so that fewer strings are struck for each note

soft-shoe *adj*
of or being tap dancing done in soft-soled shoes without metal taps

soh, so /soh/ *n*
the 5th note of the diatonic scale in solmization

Sokolova, Lydia /sokə'lohvə/
née *Hilda Munnings* (1896–1974) English ballet dancer

sol /sol/ *n*
so

solenne /ˌsoh'lenay/ *adv or adj*
in a solemn manner – **solennemente** *adv*

sol-fa /'sol ˌfah/ *n*
1 *also* **sol-fa syllables** the syllables *do, re, mi,* etc used in singing the notes of the scale
2 solmization
3 tonic sol-fa

solfège /sol'fezh/ *n*
(a singing exercise or practice in sight-reading vocal music using) the application of the sol-fa syllables to a scale or a melody

solfeggio /sol'feji·oh/ *n*
solfège

solmization /ˌsolmie'zaysh(ə)n/ *n*
the act, practice, or system of using syllables to denote notes or the degrees of a scale

solo /'sohloh/ *n, pl* **solos**
a (composition for) performance by a single voice or instrument with or without accompaniment – **solo** *adj,* **soloist** *n*

solo organ *n*
a division of a pipe organ consisting of stops with an individual character suitable for solo effects

Solti, Sir Georg /'sholti/
(born 1912) British (Hungarian-born) conductor

Somes, Michael George /sohmz/
(born 1917) English dancer and ballet director

sonata /sə'nahtə/ *n*
an instrumental composition typically for 1 or 2 players and of 3 or 4 movements in contrasting forms and keys

sonata form *n*
a musical form that is used esp for the first movement of a sonata, symphony, concerto, etc and consists basically of an exposition, a development, and a recapitulation in which

usu 2 themes are introduced, developed, and then repeated
– called also FIRST MOVEMENT FORM

sonatina /ˌsonəˈteenə/ n
a short usu simplified sonata

song /song/ n
1 the act, art, or product of singing
2 (the melody of) a short composition usu with words

song cycle n
a group of related songs designed to form a musical entity

songster /ˈsongstə/ , *feminine* **songstress** /-stris/ n
a skilled singer

songwriter /-ˌrietə/ n
a person who composes words or music for (popular) songs
– **songwriting** n

sonorous /ˈsonərəs, ˈsoh-/ adj
giving out sound (e g when struck) – **sonorously** adv,
sonorousness n, **sonority** n

sopranino /ˌsoprəˈneenoh/ n, pl **sopraninos**
an instrument (e g a recorder or saxophone) higher in pitch
than the soprano

soprano /səˈprahnoh/ n, pl **sopranos**
1 the highest part in 4-part harmony
2 (a person with) the highest singing voice of women, boys,
or castrati
3 a member of a family of instruments having the highest
range – **soprano** adj

sordino /sawˈdeenoh/ n, pl **sordini** /-ni/
a mute <*con sordini*>

sospirando /ˌsospiˈrandoh/ adv or adj
sighingly; in a plaintive style

sostenuto /ˌsostəˈnyoohtoh/ adj or adv
sustained

sostenuto pedal n
an optional third pedal on a piano that enables the

performer to sustain selected notes

sotto voce /ˌsotoh 'vohchi/ *adv or adj*

at a very low volume

soul /sohl/ *n*

music that originated in American negro gospel singing, is closely related to rhythm and blues, and is characterized by intensity of feeling and earthiness – **souled** *adj*

soundboard /'sownd,bawd/ *n*

a thin resonant board so placed in an instrument as to reinforce its sound by sympathetic vibration

sound bow /boh/ *n*

the thick part of a bell against which the clapper strikes

sound box *n*

the hollow resonating chamber in the body of an instrument (e g a violin)

sound hole *n*

an opening in the soundboard of an instrument for increasing resonance

sounding board *n*

a soundboard

soundpost *n*

a small post in an instrument of the viol or violin family, set nearly under the bridge as a support and as a transmitter of vibrations

Sousa, John Philip /'soohzə, 'soohsə/

the '*March King*' (1854–1932) American bandmaster and composer

sousaphone /'soohzə,fohn/ *n*

a large tuba that has a flared adjustable bell, is designed to encircle the player and rest on the left shoulder, and is used primarily in American marching bands

space /spays/ *n*

any of the degrees between or above or below the lines of a staff – see illustration at MUSIC

spiccato /spi'kahtoh/ *n or adj, pl* **spiccatos**
(a technique, performance, or passage) played using the bow so that it rebounds from the string

spinet /'spinit, spi'net/ *n*
a small keyboard instrument of the harpsichord type having the strings at an angle to the keyboard

spiritoso /ˌspiri'tohsoh, -zoh/ *adv or adj*
animated, spirited

spiritual /'spirichooəl/ *n*
a usu emotional religious song of a kind performed esp among negroes in the southern USA

splits /splits/ *n taking sing or pl vb*
the act of lowering oneself to the floor or leaping into the air with legs extended at right angles to the trunk

Spohr, Louis /shpaw/
(1784–1859) German composer, violinist, and conductor; works include much chamber music and opera

springar /'spring·gah/ *n*
a Norwegian dance in triple time, danced by 2 people

springdans /'spring,dahn(t)s/ *n*
a Norwegian leaping dance for men

square dance *n*
a dance for 4 couples who form a hollow square – **square dancer** *n*, **square dancing** *n*

square piano *n*
an early piano that has an oblong case and is horizontally strung

squeeze-box /'skweez,boks/ *n*
an accordion

stacc. *adv or adj*
staccato

staccatissimo /ˌstakə'tisimoh/ *adv or adj*
in a sharper and more detached staccato manner

staccato /stə'kahtoh/ *n, adv, or adj, pl* **staccatos**

(a manner of speaking or performing, or a piece of music performed) in a sharp, disconnected, or abrupt way

staccato mark *n*

a pointed vertical stroke or a dot placed over or under a note to be produced staccato – see illustration at DIRECTION

staff /stahf/ *n, pl* **staffs, staves** /stayvz/

a set of usu 5 parallel horizontal lines on which music is written – see illustration at MUSIC

Stainer, John /'staynə/

(1840–1901) English organist, composer, and writer of textbooks

standard /'standəd/ *n*

a composition, specif a popular song, that has become a part of the established repertoire

Stanford, Sir Charles Villiers /'stanfəd/

(1852–1924) Irish composer of orchestral and chamber music, oratorios, operas, songs, and church music; works include the service for the Anglican church known as *Stanford in B flat*

stanza /'stanzə/ *n*

a division of a poem or song consisting of a series of lines arranged together in a usu recurring pattern of metre and rhyme – **stanzaic** *adj*

Starr, Ringo /stah/

pseudonym of *Richard Starkey* (born 1940) English drummer; member of the *Beatles*

statement /'staytmənt/ *n*

the presentation of a theme in a composition

stave /stayv/ *n*

a staff

steel band *n*

a band that plays tuned percussion instruments cut out of oil drums, developed originally in Trinidad – **steelbandsman** *n*

steel guitar *n*

a usu electric instrument with steel strings that are plucked while being pressed with a movable steel bar

stem /stem/ *n*
the main vertical stroke of a printed note – **stemless** *adj*, **stemmed** *adj*

step[1] /step/ *n*
a combination of foot (and body) movements constituting a unit or a repeated pattern <*a dance* ~> – **steplike** *adj*, **stepped** *adj*

step[2] *vi*
to dance

step dance *n*
a dance in which steps are emphasized rather than gesture or posture

Stern, Isaac /stuhn/
(born 1920) American (Russian-born) violinist

stick /stik/ *n*
1 a conductor's baton
2 a violin bow

stock /stok/ *n*
any of the short tubes in a bagpipe which are inserted into the bag and hold the pipes in place

Stockhausen, Karlheinz /ˈshtokˌhowzən/
(born 1928) German composer, pioneer of electronic music; works include *Gruppen, Stimmung*

Stokowski, Leopold Antoni Stanislaw /stəˈkofski, -ˈkov-/
(1882–1977) American (British-born) conductor

stomp /stomp/ *n*
a jazz dance characterized by heavy stamping

stop[1] /stop/ *vt*
to change the pitch of
a (e g a violin string) by pressing with the finger
b (a woodwind instrument) by closing 1 or more finger holes
c (a French horn) by putting the hand into the bell

    d (e g a trumpet) by putting a mute into the bell – **stoppable** *adj*

stop² *n*

    1 (a switch or handle operating) a graduated set of organ pipes of similar design and tone quality

    2 a corresponding set of vibrators or reeds of a reed organ

Stradivari, Antonio /ˌstradiˈvahri, -ˈveəri/

    Antonius Stradivarius (1644–1737) Italian violin maker; assisted by his 2 sons **Francesco** (1671–1743) and **Omobono** (1679–1742)

straight /strayt/ *adj*

    of or being a style of jazz with a fixed melody that is played as written; cool – compare HOT

strain /strayn/ *n*, **strains** *n pl*

    a passage of verbal or musical expression

strathspey /ˌstrathˈspay/ *n*

    (the music for) a Scottish dance similar to a reel and marked by gliding steps

Straus, Oscar /s(h)trows/

    (1870–1954) Austrian composer, esp of light opera

Strauss, Johann

    father of Johann and Josef, (1804–49) Austrian conductor and composer; works include *The Radetzky March*

Strauss, Johann (the Younger)

    brother of Josef, (1825–99) Austrian violinist, conductor, and composer, esp of Viennese light music; works include 16 operettas (e g *Die Fledermaus*), waltzes, some of which (e g *The Blue Danube* and *Tales from the Vienna Woods*) are regarded as symphonic poems, polkas, galops, and other dances

Strauss, Josef

    (1827–70) Austrian composer

Strauss, Richard Georg

    (1864–1949) German composer; works include operas (e g

Der Rosenkavalier), symphonic poems (e g *Till Eulenspiegel*), and songs

Stravinsky, Igor Fedorovich /strə'vin(t)ski/
(1882–1971) Russian-born composer; works include many ballets (e g *The Firebird*, *Petrushka* and *The Rite of Spring*), operas, and orchestral, chamber, and choral music (e g *Symphony of Psalms*) – **Stravinskyan, Stravinskian** *adj*

Streisand, Barbra /'striezənd/
(born 1942) American actress and singer

strepitoso /strepi'tohsoh, -zoh/ *adv or adj*
in a noisy and impetuous manner

stress /stres/ *n*
ACCENT 1 – **stressless** *adj*

stretto¹ /'stretoh/ *n, pl* **stretti** /-ti/, **strettos**
1 the overlapping of answer with subject in a fugue
2 the part of a fugue characterized by this overlapping
3 a concluding passage performed in a quicker tempo

stretto² *adv or adj*
gradually faster; accelerando

stride piano *n*
a style of jazz piano playing in which the right hand plays the melody while the left hand alternates between a single note and a chord played an octave or more higher

strike /striek/ *vt*
to play or produce on keys or strings

strike note *n*
the note to which a bell is tuned – compare HUM NOTE

string¹ /string/ *n*
1 the gut or wire cord of a musical instrument
2 **strings** *pl*, **string** a stringed instrument of an orchestra – **stringed** *adj*, **stringless** *adj*

string² *vt*
to equip with strings

stringendo /ˌstrin'jendoh/ *adv or adj*

with quickening of tempo (e g to a climax)

strophic /'strofik, 'stroh-/ *adj*
using the same music for successive stanzas of a song

strum /strum/ *vb*
1 *vt* to brush the fingers lightly over the strings of (an instrument) in playing <~ *a guitar*>; *also* to thrum
2 *vt* to play (music) on a guitar <~ *a tune*>
3 *vi* to strum a stringed instrument – **strummer** *n*

study /'studi/ *n*
an étude

suabe flute /'swahbə/ *n*
a wood flute organ stop of 4-foot pitch with a bright clear tone

subdominant /ˌsub'dominənt/ *n*
the fourth note of a diatonic scale – called also FOURTH – **subdominant** *adj*

subinterval /ˌsub'intəv(ə)l/ *n*
an interval that is a subdivision of a larger or a major interval

subito /'soohbiˌtoh/ *adv*
immediately, suddenly

subject /'subjikt/ *n*
the principal melodic phrase on which a composition or movement is based – **subjectless** *adj*

submediant /ˌsub'meedi·ənt/ *n*
the sixth note of a diatonic scale – called also SIXTH

subtonic /ˌsub'tonik/ *n*
the leading note

suite /sweet/ *n*
1 a 17th- and 18th-c instrumental form consisting of a series of dances, esp including an allemande, courante, sarabande, and gigue
2 a modern instrumental composition in several movements of different character

3 an orchestral concert arrangement of material drawn from a longer work (e g a ballet)

Sullivan, Sir Arthur (Seymour) /'sulivən/
(1842–1900) English composer, conductor, and organist; he collaborated with Sir William Shwenck Gilbert on many popular operettas

supertonic /ˌsoohpə'tonik/ n
the second note of a diatonic scale – called also SECOND

Suppé, Franz von /'soohpay/
né *Francesco Ezechiele Ermenegildo Cavaliere Suppé-Demelli* (1819–95) Dalmatian-born composer, esp of operas and operettas

suspension /sə'spensh(ə)n/ n
(the sustaining of) 1 or more notes of a chord held over into the following chord producing a momentary discord

Susskind, (Jan) Walter /'suskint/
(1918–80) British (Czech-born) conductor

sustaining pedal n
a pedal on a piano that holds off the dampers, allowing the notes to be sustained; often wrongly called 'loud pedal'

Sutherland, Dame Joan /'suthəˌlənd/
(born 1926) Australian soprano

swell /swel/ n
1 a gradual increase and decrease of the loudness of a sound
2 a device used in an organ for governing loudness

swell box n
a box or chamber in an organ that contains the reeds or a set of pipes and has shutters that open or shut usu by means of a pedal in order to regulate the volume

swell organ, swell n
a division in a pipe organ in which the pipes are enclosed in a swell box

swell pedal n
a pedal that operates an organ swell usu by working a

balanced lever mechanism that opens or shuts the louvres of
the swell box

swing¹ /swing/ *vb*

1 *vt* to play or sing (e g a melody) in the style of swing music
2 *vi* to play or sing with a lively compelling rhythm; *specif* to
play swing music – **swingable** *adj*, **swinger** *n*

swing² *n*

1 a sweeping or rhythmic movement of the body or a bodily
part
2 jazz played usu by a large dance band and characterized
by a strong rigid unvarying rhythm, simple harmony, and a
basic melody using a free rubato and usu submerged in
improvisation – **swing** *adj*

sword dance *n*

a dance performed over, round, or brandishing swords; *esp*
a Scottish-Highland solo dance usu performed in the angles
formed by 2 swords crossed on the ground – **sword dancer** *n*

sympathetic /ˌsimpəˈthetik/ *adj*

relating to sounds produced, or strings sounded, by
sympathetic vibration – **sympathetically** *adv*

sympathetic vibration *n*

a vibration produced in one body by vibrations of the same
period in another

symphonic /simˈfonik/ *adj*

relating to or having the form or character of a symphony
<~ *music*> – **symphonically** *adv*

symphonic poem *n*

an extended orchestral composition, based on a legend,
tale, etc and freer in form than a symphony

symphonist /ˈsimfənist/ *n*

a composer of symphonies

symphony /ˈsimfəni/ *n*

1a a usu long and complex sonata for symphony orchestra
1b a composition of similar proportions

2 *chiefly NAm* a symphony orchestra

symphony orchestra *n*
a large orchestra of wind instruments, strings, and percussion

syncopate /'singkə,payt/ *vt*
to modify or affect (rhythm) by syncopation – **syncopator** *n*

syncopation /,singkə'paysh(ə)n/ *n*
(a rhythm or passage characterized by) a temporary displacement of the regular metrical accent caused typically by stressing the weak beat – **syncopative** *adj*

synthes·izer, -iser /'sinthə,siezə/ *n*
an extremely versatile electronic instrument that produces a sound that can be altered in many ways (e g to mimic other instruments) and is usu played by means of a keyboard

Szell, George /sel, zel/
(1897–1970) American (Hungarian-born) conductor

Szeryng, Henryk /'shering/
(born 1918) Polish-born violinist

Szymanowski, Karol /,shimə'nofski/
(1882–1937) Polish composer; works include operas, concertos, and symphonies

T

tabla /'tahblə/ *n*

a pair of small hand drums of different sizes used esp in Indian classical music

tablature /'tabləchə/ *n*

an instrumental notation indicating the string, fret, keys, or fingering to be used instead of the note to be sounded

tabor *also* **tabour** /'taybə/ *n*

a small drum with 1 head of soft calfskin used to accompany a pipe or fife played by the same person

taboret /'taybərit/ *n*

a tabor

tacet /'tayset/

– used to indicate that a particular instrument is not to play during a movement or long section

Taglioni, Filippo /ˌtali'ohni/

(1777–1871) Italian ballet dancer and choreographer

Taglioni, Maria

daughter of Filippo, (1804–84) Italian ballet dancer

Tailleferre, Germaine /'tie,yə,feə/

(1892–1983) French pianist and composer

tailpiece /'tayl,pees/ *n*

a triangular piece from which the strings of a stringed instrument are stretched to the pegs

Takemitsu, Toru /ˌtake'mitsooh/

(born 1930) Japanese composer; works incorporate Japanese and European elements

tala /'tahlə/ *n*

any of the ancient traditional rhythmic patterns of Indian music

Tallis, Thomas /'talis/

(1505–85) English organist and composer, esp of church

music

tambour /'tambooə/ *n*

a drum

tamboura, tambura /tam'booərə/ *n*

an Asian stringed instrument used to produce a drone
accompaniment to singing

tambourin /'tambə,ran(h)/ *n*

1 a long narrow drum used in Provence
2 a lively old Provençal dance originally with tambourin
accompaniment; *also* music written for this dance in quick
duple time usu with a drone bass on the tonic or dominant

tambourine /,tambə'reen/ *n*

a shallow single-headed drum with loose metallic discs at
the sides that is held in the hand and played by shaking,
striking with the hand, or rubbing with the thumb

tam-tam /'tam ,tam/ *n*

a gong

tangent /'tanjənt/ *n*

an upright flat-ended metal pin at the inner end of a
clavichord key that strikes the string to produce the note

tango /'tang·goh/ *n, pl* **tangos**

(the music for) a ballroom dance of Latin-American origin
in $\frac{4}{4}$ time, characterized by long pauses and stylized body
positions – **tango** *vi*

tantara /'tantərə, tan'tahrə/ *n*

the blare of a trumpet or horn

tanto /'tantoh/ *adv*

much; so much <*allegro non* ~>

tap¹ /'tap/ *n*

a small piece of metal attached to the sole or heel of
tap-dancing shoes

tap² *n*

any of several usu rapid drumbeats on a snare drum

tap dance *n*

a step dance tapped out audibly by means of shoes with hard soles or soles and heels to which taps have been added – **tap-dance** *vi*, **tap dancer** *n*, **tap dancing** *n*

tarantella /ˌtarən'telə/, **tarantelle** /-el/ *n*
(music in § time that usu alternates between major and minor keys and is suitable for) a vivacious folk dance of southern Italy

Tartini, Giuseppe /tah'teeni/
(1692–1770) Italian violinist and composer; founder of school of violin playing; works include concertos and sonatas (e g *Devil's Trill*)

tasto solo /ˌtastoh 'sohloh/ *n*
– used as a direction in keyboard music in connection with a figured bass to indicate that the bass is to be played alone, without harmony

Tate, Phyllis /tayt/
(born 1911) English composer

tattoo¹ /ta'tooh/ *n, pl* **tattoos**
a rapid rhythmic beating or rapping

tattoo² *vb*
1 *vt* to beat or rap rhythmically on; drum on
2 *vi* to give a series of rhythmic taps

Tatum, Arthur /'taytəm/
'*Art*' (1910–56) American jazz pianist

Tauber, Richard /'towbə/
(1891–1948) British (Austrian-born) tenor

Taverner, John /'tavənə/
(c1490–1545) English composer, esp of sacred music

Taylor, Cecil /'taylə/
(born 1933) American jazz pianist

Tchaikovsky, Pyotr Ilyich /chie'kofski, -'kov-/
(1840–93) Russian composer; works include 6 symphonies, operas (e g *Eugene Onegin*), concertos, ballets (e g *Nutcracker*), chamber music, piano compositions, and songs

– **Tchaikovskyan, Tchaikovskian** *adj*

te, ti /tee/ *n*
the 7th note of the diatonic scale in solmization

Te Deum /,tay 'dayəm, ,tee 'dee-/ *n, pl* **Te Deums**
(a musical setting of) a Christian hymn of praise to God

Te Kanawa, Dame Kiri /,tay ka'nahwə/
(born 1944) New Zealand soprano

Telemann, Georg Philipp /'taylə,man/
(1681–1767) German composer, one of the most prolific
ever; works include oratorios, cantatas, and chamber music

telyn /'telən/ *n*
the Welsh harp

temper /'tempə/ *vt*
to adjust the pitch of (a note, chord, or instrument) to a
temperament – **temperable** *adj*, **temperer** *n*

temperament /'temprəmənt/ *n*
the modification of the intervals of the pure scale to
produce a set of 12 fixed notes to the octave which enables a
keyboard instrument to play in more than 1 key

tempo /'tempoh/ *n, pl* **tempi** /-pi/, **tempos**
the speed of a piece or passage indicated by any of a series
of directions and often by an exact metronome marking

ten. *adv or adj*
tenuto

teneramente /,tenərə'mentay, -ti/ *adv or adj*
tenderly

tenor /'tenə/ *n*
1 the next to the lowest part in 4-part harmony
2 (someone with) the highest natural adult male singing
voice
3 a member of a family of instruments having a range next
lower than that of the alto – **tenor** *adj*

tenor clef *n*
a C clef placed so as to designate the fourth line of the staff

as middle C – see illustration at MUSIC

tenoroon /ˌtenəˈroohn/ *n*
a small bassoon pitched a fourth or fifth higher than the ordinary instrument and now virtually obsolete

tenuto /teˈnyoohtoh/ *adv or adj*
in a manner so as to hold a note or chord to its full value

ternary form /ˈtɜrnəri/ *n*
1 a form (e g a rondo) in which the principal subject appears 3 or more times
2 a form in which the third part is a repetition of the first with a contrasting section in the middle

terpsichorean /ˌtuhpsikəˈree-ən, ˌtuhpsiˈkawri-ən/ *adj*
of dancing

Tertis, Lionel /ˈtuhtis/
(1876–1975) English viola player

tessitura /ˌtesəˈt(y)oоərə/ *n*
the part of the register in which most of the notes of a melody or voice part lie or in which a voice or instrument naturally sounds its best

tetrachord /ˈtetrəˌkawd/ *n*
a diatonic series of 4 notes with an interval of a perfect fourth between the first and last

tetralogy /teˈtraləji/ *n*
a series of 4 connected works

texture /ˈtekschə/ *n*
a pattern of sound created by notes or lines played or sung together – **textural** *adj*, **textured** *adj*

Teyte, Dame Maggie /tayt/
Dame Margaret Cottingham (1888–1976) English soprano

Thalben-Ball, Sir George (Thomas) /ˌthalbənˈbawl/
(born 1896) British (Australian-born) organist and composer

theme /theem/ *n*
a melodic subject of a composition or movement

theme song *n*
  1 a recurring melody in a musical play or in a film that characterizes the production or one of its characters
  2 a signature tune

Theodorakis, Mikis /ˌt(h)ayohdəˈrahkis/
  (born 1925) Greek composer

theorbo /thiˈawboh/ *n, pl* **theorbos**
  a 17th-c instrument like a large lute but having an extra set of bass strings

third¹ /thuhd/ *adj or n*
  (related to or having) a part typically subordinate to or lower in pitch than the second part in concerted or ensemble music

third² *n*
  1 (the harmonic combination of 2 notes at) an interval of 3 diatonic degrees
  2 a note separated by this interval from a root; *specif* the mediant

thirty-second note *n*
  NAm a demisemiquaver

thirty-second rest *n*
  NAm a rest of the same time value as a thirty-second note

thirty-two-foot stop, 32-foot stop *n*
  a pipe-organ stop sounding pitches 2 octaves lower than the notes indicate – compare EIGHT-FOOT STOP

Thomson, Virgil Garnett /ˈtom(p)sən/
  (born 1896) American composer and critic

thoroughbass /ˈthurəˌbays/ *n*
  a continuo

threnode /ˈthrenohd, ˈthree-/ *n*
  a threnody – **threnodist** *n*, **threnodic** *adj*

threnody /ˈthrenədi, ˈthree-/ *n*
  a song of lamentation, esp for the dead

through-composed /ˌthroohkəmˈpohzd/ *adj*

of a song having new music provided for each stanza

thrum /thrum/ *vb*

to play (e g a stringed instrument) in an idle or relaxed manner

thump /thump/ *vt*

to produce (music) mechanically or in a mechanical manner <~ed *out a tune on the piano*> – **thumper** *n*

ti /tee/ *n*

te

Tibbett, Lawrence Mervil /'tibet/

(1896–1960) American baritone

tie¹ /tie/ *n*

a curved line that joins 2 notes of the same pitch to denote a single sustained note with the time value of the 2 – see illustration at DIRECTION – **tieless** *adj*

tie² *vt*

to unite (notes) by a tie

Tieffenbrucker /'teefən,broohkə/

German family of stringed instrument makers: esp **Gaspar** (1514–71) who made lutes and viols famous for their exquisite inlaid work

tight /tiet/ *adj*

playing in unison – **tightly** *adv*, **tightness** *n*

Tilley, Vesta /'tili/

pseudonym of *Lady de Frece*, née *Matilda Alice Powles* (1864–1952) English music-hall entertainer

timbre /'tambə, 'timbə, 'tahmbə/ *also* **timber** /'timbə/ *n*

the quality given to a sound by its overtones; *specif* the quality of tone distinctive of a particular singing voice or musical instrument

timbrel /'timbrəl/ *n*

a small hand drum or tambourine

time /tiem/ *n*

1 a tempo

2 the grouping of the beats of music; a rhythm, metre

time signature *n*

a sign placed on a staff being usu a fraction whose denominator indicates the kind of note taken as the time unit for the beat (e g 4 for a crotchet or 8 for a quaver) and whose numerator indicates the number of beats per bar – see illustration

timpani /ˈtimpəni/ *n taking sing or pl vb*

a set of 2 or 3 kettledrums played by 1 performer (e g in an orchestra) – **timpanist** *n*

Tin Pan Alley *n*

a district that is a centre for composers and publishers of popular music; *also, taking sing or pl vb* the body of such composers and publishers

tintinnabulation /ˌtintiˌnabyooˈlaysh(ə)n/ *n*

1 the ringing of bells

2 a sound as if of bells – **tintinnabulary** *adj*

tin whistle *n*

a small instrument usu made of metal related to the recorder and having 6 finger holes

Tippett, Sir Michael Kemp /ˈtipit/

(born 1905) English composer; works include 4 operas, the oratorio *A Child of Our Time*, concertos and other orchestral pieces, chamber and piano music, and song cycles

toccata /təˈkahtə/ *n*

a composition in a free style and characterized by rapid runs, usu for keyboard instrument

Tommasini, Vincenzo /ˌtoməˈzini/

(1878–1950) Italian composer

tom-tom /tom/ *n*

a usu long and narrow small-headed drum commonly beaten with the hands

tonal /ˈtohn(ə)l/ *adj*

having tonality – **tonally** *adv*

Simple Time

Duple

Quadruple

Each Simple Time has a corresponding Compound Time.

Triple

Compound Time

Duple

Quadruple

Triple

These are the most common time signatures. These are infinite combinations.

tonality /toh'naləti/ *n*
1 KEY 3
2 the organization of all the notes and chords of a piece of music in relation to a tonic

tone /tohn/ *n*
1 a sound of a definite frequency with relatively weak overtones
2 a whole tone
3 *chiefly NAm* NOTE 1

tone cluster *n*
a combination of dissonant notes, usu one tone apart from each other, which are played together by one or more instruments

tone poem *n*
a symphonic poem – **tone poet** *n*

tone-row /roh/ *n*
chiefly NAm note row

tongue[1] /'tung/ *n*
1 the free vibrating end of the reed in an organ pipe or wind instrument
2 the vibrating part of a Jew's harp

tongue[2] *vb*
to articulate notes on a wind instrument by successively interrupting the stream of wind with the action of the tongue

tonic[1] /'tonik/ *adj*
of or based on the first note of a scale – **tonically** *adv*

tonic[2] *n*
the first note of a diatonic scale; a keynote

tonic sol-fa *n*
a system of solmization that replaces the normal notation with sol-fa syllables

Tortelier, Paul /ˌtaw'teli·ay/
(born 1914) French cellist and composer

Toscanini, Arturo /ˌtoskəˈneeni/
(1867–1957) Italian conductor

tosto /ˈtohstoh/ *adv or adj*
at a rapid tempo

touch /tuch/ *n*
1 a manner or method of touching or striking esp the keys of a keyboard instrument
2 the relative resistance to pressure of the keys of a keyboard (e g of a piano)

tour en l'air /ˌtooə on ˈlayə/ *n, pl* **tours en l'air** /∼/
a turn in ballet made while leaping vertically upwards into the air

Tourte, François /ˈtoohət/
(1747–1835) French craftsman responsible for the design of the modern violin bow

tranquillo /ˌtranˈkwiloh/ *adv or adj*
in a quiet or calm manner

transcribe /tranˈskrieb; *also* trahn-/ *vt*
to make a transcription of – **transcriber** *n*

transcription /tranˈskripsh(ə)n, trahn-/ *n*
1 an often free arrangement of a composition for some instrument or voice other than the original
2 a version in a different form of notation from the one in which a piece of music was written – **transcriptional** *adj*

transition /tranˈzish(ə)n, trahn-/ *n*
1 a modulation
2 a passage leading from one section of a piece to another – **transitional** *adj*, **transitionally** *adv*

transpose /tranˈspohz, trahn-/ *vb*
to write or perform (music) in a different key – **transposable** *adj*

traps /traps/ *n pl*
a group of percussion instruments (e g rattles and drums) used esp in a dance or jazz band

traurig /'trow͵rikh/ *adv or adj*
sadly

treble¹ /'trebl/ *n*
1 the highest voice part in harmonic music; a soprano; *also* someone, esp a boy, who performs this part
2 the upper half of the whole vocal or instrumental tonal range – compare BASS
3 a member of a family of instruments having the highest range

treble² *adj*
relating to or having the range or part of a treble – **trebly** *adv*

treble clef *n*
1 a clef that places the note G above middle C on the second line of the staff – called also G CLEF; compare BASS CLEF; see illustration at MUSIC
2 the treble staff

tre corde /͵tray 'kawday/ *adv or adj*
with the soft pedal released

trem. *adv or adj*
tremolando

tremolando¹ *also* **tremulando** /͵tremə'landoh/ *adv or adj*
tremulous

tremolando² *also* **tremulando** *n, pl* **tremolandos, tremolandi** /-di/
a tremolo effect esp by the strings of an orchestra

tremolo /'treməloh/ *n, pl* **tremolos**
1a the rapid reiteration of a note or of alternating notes to produce a tremulous effect
1b a perceptible rapid variation of pitch in the (singing) voice; vibrato
2 a mechanical device in an organ for causing a tremulous effect

tremulant /'tremyoolənt/ *n*

a device to impart a vibration giving a sound a tremulous effect; an organ stop

trepak /trə'pok, tray-/ *n*

a fiery Ukrainian folk dance in duple time performed by men and featuring the leg-flinging prisiadka

triad /'trie,ad/ *n*

a chord of 3 notes consisting of a root with its third and fifth and constituting the harmonic basis of tonal music – **triadic** *adj*

triangle /'trie,ang·gl/ *n*

a percussion instrument consisting of a steel rod bent into the form of a triangle open at 1 angle and sounded by striking with a small metal rod

trichord /'trie,kawd/ *n*

any of the triple strings of a piano that produce notes in the top range – compare BICHORD

trill¹ /tril/ *n*

the alternation of a note with the one above it – called also SHAKE; see illustration at DIRECTION

trill² *vt*

to utter as or with a trill <~ *the* r> – **triller** *n*

trio /'tree·oh/ *n, pl* **trios**

1 (a composition for) 3 instruments, voices, or performers
2 the secondary or episodic division of a minuet, scherzo, etc
3 a group of 3 performers

trionfale /,trion'fahlay/ *adv or adj*

in a triumphant manner

trionfante /,trion'fantay/ *adv or adj*

trionfale

triple /tripl/ *adj*

marked by 3 beats per bar <~ *metre*>

triple counterpoint *n*

3-part counterpoint so written that any part may be played

above or below any other

triplet /'triplit/ *n*

a group of 3 notes performed in the time of 2 or 4 of the same value

triple-tongue *vi*

to use tongue movements to produce a very fast succession of detached notes on a wind instrument

tritone /'trie,tohn/ *n*

an interval of 3 whole tones

troll /trohl, trol/ *vb*

1 *vt* to sing loudly

2 *vi* to sing or play an instrument in a jovial manner

trombone /trom'bohn/ *n*

1 a brass instrument consisting of a long cylindrical metal tube with a movable slide for varying the pitch and a usual range 1 octave lower than that of the trumpet

2 a large-scale pipe-organ stop of a sound quality similar to that of a trombone – **trombonist** *n*

troppo /'tropoh/ *adv or adj*

too much

troubadour /'troohbǝdaw, -dooǝ/ *n*

a lyric poet or poet-musician, chiefly in southern France in the 11th to 13th c, who wrote in Provençal mainly about courtly love

troupe /troohp/ *n*

a company or troop of theatrical performers

trouvère /'trooh,veǝ/ *n*

the central and northern French counterpart of a troubadour

trump /trump/ *n*

a trumpet (call)

trumpet¹ /'trumpit/ *n*

1 a wind instrument consisting of a usu metal tube, a cup-shaped mouthpiece, and a flared bell; *specif* a valved

brass instrument having a cylindrical tube and a usual range
from F sharp below middle C upwards for 2 octaves
2 a musical instrument (e g a cornet) that resembles a
trumpet
3 an 8-foot pipe-organ reed stop with a penetrating tone –
trumpetlike *adj*

trumpet² *vi*
to blow a trumpet

trumpeter /'trumpitə/ *n*
a trumpet player; *specif* one who gives (military) signals
with a trumpet

tuba /'tyoohbə/ *n*
a large brass instrument having valves, a conical tube, a
cup-shaped mouthpiece, and a usual range an octave lower
than that of the euphonium

tube /tyoohb/ *n*
the basically cylindrical section between the mouthpiece and
bell of a wind instrument – **tubelike** *adj*

tubular bells *n taking sing or pl vb*
a percussion instrument composed of a series of brass or
steel tubes of varying lengths hanging in a frame and giving
a range of 1½ octaves

tucket /'tukit/ *n*
archaic a fanfare on a trumpet

Tudor, Antony /'tyoohdə/
(born 1908) English ballet dancer and choreographer

tune¹ /tyoohn/ *n*
1a a pleasing succession of notes; a melody
1b the predominant melody in a composition
2 correct pitch (with another instrument, voice, etc)

tune² *vt*
to adjust the pitch of; *esp* to cause to be in tune – **tunable,
tuneable** *adj*, **tuner** *n*

tuneless /'tyoohnlis/ *adj*

without an intended or recognizable melody; not tuneful –
tunelessly *adv*, **tunelessness** *n*

tuning fork /'tyoohning/ *n*
a 2-pronged metal implement that gives a fixed note when
struck and is useful for tuning instruments and setting
pitches for singing

tuning pin *n*
a wrest pin

turn /tuhn/ *n*
1 any of various rotating or pivoting movements in dancing
2 an ornament played on the principal note and the notes
next above and below – see illustration at DIRECTION

tutta forza /ˌtootə 'fawtsə/ *adv or adj*
with the whole power; as loud as possible

tutti /'toohti/ *n, adj, or adv*
(a passage or section to be) performed by all the performers

tutu /'tooh,tooh/ *n*
a very short projecting stiff skirt worn by a ballerina

twang¹ /twang/ *n*
a harsh quick ringing sound like that of a plucked string

twang² *vb*
1 *vi* to sound with a twang
2 *vt* to cause to sound with a twang
3 *vt* to pluck the strings of

twelve-note *adj*
of or being serial music based on a note-row

twelve-tone *adj*
twelve-note

twist¹ /twist/ *vi*
to dance the twist

twist² *n*
a dance popular esp in the 1960s and performed with
gyrations, esp of the hips

two-foot stop, 2-foot stop *n*

a pipe-organ stop sounding pitches 2 octaves higher than the notes indicate – compare EIGHT-FOOT STOP

two-step *n*

(a piece of music for) a ballroom dance in duple time

two-tone *adj*

of or being popular music played by groups consisting of black, esp West Indian, and white musicians and including elements of reggae and new wave – **two-tone** *n*

U

ukulele /ˌyoohkəˈlayli/ *n*
a small usu 4-stringed guitar of Portuguese origin

una corda /ˌoohnə ˈkawdə/ *adv or adj*
with the soft pedal of a piano depressed

unison /ˈyoohnis(ə)n, -z(ə)n/ *n*
1 sounding the same note
2 the writing, playing, or singing of parts in a passage at the same pitch or in octaves – **unison** *adj*

upbeat /ˈupˌbeet/ *n*
an unaccented (e g the last) beat in a bar, when the conductor's baton is moving upwards before the main beat

up-bow /ˈupˌboh/ *n*
a stroke in playing a bowed instrument (e g a violin) in which the bow is moved across the strings from the tip to the heel

upper partial *n*
an overtone

upright, upright piano *n*
a piano with vertical frame and strings

up-tempo /ˈtempoh/ *adj or n*
(played at) a fast-moving tempo (e g in jazz)

ut /ut, ooht/ *n*
doh – used in French fixed-doh solmization to refer not to the 1st note of any scale, but to the note C in whatever scale or context it may occur

V

valeta /vəˈleetə/ *n*
a veleta

valse /vals/ *n*
a (concert) waltz

value /ˈvalyooh/ *n*
the relative duration of a note

valve /valv/ *n*
a device in a brass instrument for quickly varying the tube length in order to change the fundamental note by a definite interval – **valved** *adj*, **valveless** *adj*

vamp¹ /vamp/ *n*
a simple improvised accompaniment, esp to a song

vamp² *vb*
to extemporize and improvise (an accompaniment) – **vamper** *n*

Varèse, Edgard /vəˈrayz/
(1883–1965) American (French-born) composer, esp of music incorporating novel harmonic, rhythmic, and coloristic devices

variation /ˌveəriˈaysh(ə)n/ *n*
1 the repetition of a theme with modifications in rhythm, tune, harmony, or key
2 a solo dance in ballet – **variational** *adj*, **variationally** *adv*

vaudeville /ˈvawdə,vil/ *n*
1 a street song; *broadly* any simple song
2 musical comedy
3 a long song in which all the characters take part and which forms the finale to a play or opera
4 *chiefly NAm* a music hall entertainment consisting of separate performances (e g of songs, skits, and acrobatics)

Vaughan Williams, Ralph /ˌvawnˈwilyəmz/

(1872–1958) English composer; works include many
orchestral pieces (e g *A London Symphony* and *Fantasia on
a Theme by Thomas Tallis*), choral music (e g *A Sea
Symphony*), operas, songs, and chamber music

veleta, valeta /və'leetə/ *n*
a ballroom dance of English origin in waltz time

veloce /ve'lohchay/ *adv or adj*
in a rapid tempo

Venite /vi'nieti/ *n*
(a musical setting of) a liturgical chant setting psalms 95 and
96

Verdi, Giuseppe /'veədi/
(1813–1901) Italian composer; esp of operas (e g *La
Traviata, Aida, Rigoletto*, and *Otello*) and choral works (e g
Requiem)

verismo /ˌver'izmoh/ *n*
the naturalistic school of Italian opera that flourished in the
late 19th and early 20th c and was marked by realistic
representation of contemporary everyday life

verse /vuhs/ *n*
1 a stanza
2 a passage in church music for solo voice or for 2 or more
voices (e g a quartet) as contrasted with passages to be sung
by the whole choir

verset /ˌvuh'sət/ *n*
an organ piece, originally to replace a verse of a psalm

versicle /'vuhsikl/ *n*
a short verse spoken or chanted by the priest and responded
to by the choir and/or congregation

version /'vuhsh(ə)n, -zh(ə)n/ *n*
an arrangement of a composition – **versional** *adj*

vibes /viebz/ *n taking sing or pl vb*
a vibraphone – **vibist** *n*

vibraphone /'viebrəˌfohn/ *n*

a percussion instrument resembling the xylophone but
having metal bars and motor-driven resonators for
sustaining its sound and producing a vibrato – **vibraphonist**
n

vibrato /vi'brahtoh/ *n, pl* **vibratos**
a slightly tremulous effect imparted to tone to add
expressiveness, by slight and rapid variations in pitch

Vickers, Jon /'vikəz/
(born 1926) Canadian tenor

Victoria, Thomás Luis de /vik'tawri·ə/
(1548–1611) Spanish composer, esp of unaccompanied
church music

vigoroso /ˌvigə'rohsoh, -zoh/ *adv or adj*
energetic in style

vihuela /vee'waylə/ *n*
a Renaissance Spanish stringed instrument having the body
of a guitar and strings tuned like those of a lute

Villa-Lobos, Heitor /ˌvilə'lohbos/
(1887–1959) Brazilian composer; wrote over 2000 works,
including operas, orchestral music (e g *Bachianas
brasileiras*), chamber, choral, and piano music, and songs

viol /'vie·əl/ *n*
any of a family of bowed stringed instruments chiefly of the
16th and 17th c with usu 6 strings and a fretted fingerboard,
played resting on or between the player's knees

viola /vi'ohlə/ *n*
an instrument of the violin family that is intermediate in size
and range between the violin and cello and is tuned a 5th
below the violin – **violist** *n*

viola da braccio /viˌohlə də 'brachioh/ *n, pl* **viole da braccio**
/viˌohlay/
a member of the early violin family; *esp* a viola

viola da gamba /'gambə/ *n, pl* **viole da gamba**
a bass member of the viol family having a range like that of

the cello

viola d'amore /da'mawri/ *n, pl* **viole d'amore**
a bowed stringed instrument which is related to the viol
family but has no frets and is played under the chin

violin /ˌvie·ə'lin/ *n*
1 a bowed stringed instrument having a fingerboard with no
frets, 4 strings, and a usual range from G below middle C
upwards for more than 4 octaves
2 an 8-foot labial pipe-organ stop having a tone like a violin
– **violinist** *n*

violoncello /ˌvie·ələn'cheloh/ *n*
a cello – **violoncellist** *n*

virginal /'vuhjinl/ *n*, **virginals** *n taking sing or pl vb*
a small rectangular keyboard instrument of the harpsichord
type popular in the 16th and 17th c

Virginia reel *n*
an American country dance

virtuoso /ˌvuhtyooh'ohsoh, -zoh/ *n, pl* **virtuosos, virtuosi** /-si,
-zi/
one who excels in the technique of an art, esp in musical
performance – **virtuosic** *adj*

vite /'veet/ *adv or adj*
quickly, lively

vivace /ˌvi'vahchay, -chi/ *adv or adj*
in a brisk spirited manner

vivacissimo /ˌvivə'chisimoh/ *adv or adj*
in a very lively or vivacious manner

Vivaldi, Antonio /vi'valdi, -'vol-/
(1678–1741) Italian violinist and composer; works include
nearly 400 concertos (e g the 4 known as *The Seasons*),
operas, and choral music

vivo /'vivoh/ *adv or adj*
vivace

vocal¹ /'vohkl/ *adj*

of, composed or arranged for, or sung by the human voice –
vocally *adv*, **vocality** *n*

vocal² *n*

a usu accompanied composition or passage for the voice

vocalise /ˌvohkəˈleez/ *n*

a wordless composition for solo voice

vocalism /ˈvohkl̩ˌiz(ə)m/ *n*

vocal art or technique in singing

vocalist /ˈvohkl̩·ist/ *n*

a singer

vocal·ize, -ise /ˈvohkəˌliez/ *vb*

1 *vt* to give voice to; utter; *specif* to sing

2 *vi* to utter vocal sounds

3 *vi* to sing (without words) – **vocalizer** *n*, **vocalization** *n*

vocal score *n*

a score for a choral work or opera comprising all vocal parts
with the orchestral parts reduced to a piano version

voce /ˈvohˌchay/ *n*

the voice

voice¹ /voys/ *n*

1 (the use, esp in singing or acting, of) sound produced by
the vocal cords and resonated by the cavities of the head,
throat, lungs, etc

2 the power or ability to sing

3 any of the melodic parts in a vocal or instrumental
composition

4 condition of the vocal organs with respect to singing <*be
in good* ~>

voice² *vt*

to adjust (e g an organ pipe) in manufacture, for producing
the proper sounds

voix céleste /ˌvwah səˈlest/ *n, pl* **voix célestes** /~/

a labial organ stop of 8-foot pitch with its characteristic soft
tremulous tone produced either by the stop being used with

another stop of slightly different pitch or by its being
composed of 2 or 3 ranks of pipes tuned sharp or flat with
each other

volante /ˌvohˈlantay/ *adv or adj*
fast and light

volkslied /ˈfolksˌleet/ *n*
a folk song

volta /ˈvohltə, ˈvoltə/ *n*
an early French couple dance characterized by pivoting and
high springs or bounds

volti subito /ˌvohlti ˈsoohbitoh/ *vb imperative*
turn over the page quickly

volume /ˈvolyoohm, ˈvolyoom/ *n*
the degree of loudness or the intensity of a sound – **volumed**
adj

voluntary *n*
an organ piece played before or after a religious service

vox coelestis /ˌvox ˌseeˈlestis/ *n*
a voix céleste

v.s. *vb imperative, often cap V&S*
volti subito

W

Wagner, (Wilhelm) Richard /ˈvahgnə/
(1813–83) German composer, esp of operas for which he
wrote both the words and the music and which showed a
new conception of opera as music drama, using leitmotifs;
works include *The Flying Dutchman*, the 4-part *Ring of the
Nibelung*, *The Mastersingers*, *Tristan and Isolda*, *Parsifal*,
and the *Siegfried Idyll* for orchestra

Wagnerian /vahgˈniəri·ən/ *adj*
(suggestive) of the music of Wagner, esp in grandiose scale
or dramatic intensity

Wagner tuba *n*
a brass instrument of mid to low range that somewhat
resembles the true tuba but is more closely related to the
French horn, having its funnel-shaped mouthpiece and
smooth tone

wah-wah pedal /ˈwah ˌwah/ *n*
wa-wa pedal

wait, wayte /wayt/ *n*
1 an early English town watchman or public musician who
sounded the hours of the night
2 *pl* a group who serenade for gratuities, esp at the
Christmas season; *sing* a member of such a group
3 a piece of music played by waits

waldflöte /ˈvawld,fluhtə/ , **wald flute** *n*
a soft pipe-organ flute stop of 8-foot and 4-foot pitch

Waller, Thomas /ˈwolə/
'*Fats*' (1904–43) American jazz pianist and composer

Walter, Bruno /ˈvoltə/
né Bruno Schlesinger (1876–1962) American
(German-born) conductor

Walton, Sir William Turner /ˈwawltən/

(1902–83) English composer; works include 2 symphonies, the opera *Troilus and Cressida*, concertos, the choral work *Balshazzar's Feast*, chamber music (e g *Façade*), songs, and film and incidental music

waltz¹ /'wawlts/ *n*
(music for or in the tempo of) a ballroom dance in time with strong accent on the first beat and a basic pattern of step-step-close

waltz² *vb*
to dance a waltz – **waltzer** *n*

Wanova, Galina Sergeyevna /va'nohvə/
(born 1910) Soviet ballet dancer

warble /'wawbl/ *vb*
1 *vi* to sing or sound in a trilling manner or with many turns and variations
2 *vt* to render musically, esp in an ornamented or trilling manner – **warble** *n*

Warlock, Peter /'wawlok/
pseudonym of *Philip Heseltine* (1894–1930) English writer and composer, esp of songs and chamber music

wa-wa pedal, wah-wah pedal /'wah ,wah/ *n*
an electronic device, connected to an amplifier and operated by a foot pedal, that is used (e g with an electric guitar) to produce a fluctuating muted effect

Weber, Carl Maria (Friedrich) Ernst von /'vaybə/
(1786–1826) German composer, conductor, and pianist; works include operas (e g *Oberon* and *Der Freischütz*) and choral and chamber music; founded the romantic school in German opera

Webern, Anton von /'vaybuhn/
(1883–1945) Austrian composer; works include chamber and piano music, orchestral pieces, and songs

Weill, Kurt /viel/
(1900–50) German-born conductor and composer of operas

(e g *The Threepenny Opera*) and instrumental works

Welsh harp *n*

a large harp with 3 rows of strings, 2 tuned diatonically in unison and the third row supplying the semitones – called also TELYN

whip /wip/ *n*

a percussion instrument in the form of a wooden clapper

whistle /'wisl/ *n*

a small wind instrument in which sound is produced by the forcible passage of breath through a slit in a short tube (e g of wood or metal)

whistle mouthpiece *n*

a mouthpiece (e g of a recorder) consisting of a whistle through which air is forced and is made to vibrate by being directed against the sharp edge of the lip

white /wiet/ *adj*

of or constituting a tone quality characterized by a controlled pure sound, a lack of warmth and colour, and a lack of resonance

whole note *n*

NAm a semibreve

whole rest *n*

NAm a rest of the same time value as a whole note

whole step *n*

NAm a whole tone

whole tone *n*

an interval (e g C-D or G-A) comprising 2 semitones; a whole-tone scale progresses only in tones

Widor, Charles Marie /vi'daw/

(1844–1937) French organist and composer

Williamson, Malcolm /'wilyəm,sən/

(born 1931) Australian composer, organist, and pianist; Master of the Queen's Music

Wilson, Sandy /'wilsən/

(born 1924) English composer and lyricist

wind¹ /wind/ n

1 wind instruments collectively, esp as distinguished from stringed and percussion instruments

2 wind, wind band *taking sing or pl vb* the group of players of such instruments

wind² /wiend/ vt

to sound (e g a call or note) on a horn

wind-chest /'wind,chest/ n

a reservoir for supplying air under pressure to the pipes or reeds of an organ

wind instrument n

an instrument (e g a trumpet, clarinet, or organ) sounded by wind; *esp* an instrument sounded by the player's breath

windway /'wind,way/ n

the narrow slit in the mouth of an organ pipe or the mouthpiece of a recorder through which the air current is directed against the lip

wolf /woolf/ n, pl **wolves** /woolvz/

1 dissonance in some chords produced on instruments with fixed notes tuned by unequal temperament (e g organs and pianos)

2 a harshness due to faulty vibration in various notes in a bowed instrument – **wolflike** adj

Wolf, Hugo /volf/

(1860–1903) Austrian composer, esp of songs

Wood, Haydn /wood/

(1881–1959) English violinist and composer

Wood, Sir Henry Joseph

(1869–1944) English conductor; inaugurated the Promenade Concerts and conducted them until his death

woodwind /-,wind/ n

1 any of a group of wind instruments (e g a clarinet, flute, or saxophone) that is characterized by a cylindrical or conical tube of wood or metal, usu with finger holes or keys, that produces notes by the vibration of a single or double reed or by the passing of air over a mouth hole **2** *taking sing or pl vb* the woodwind section of a band or orchestra

wrest pin /'rest/ *n*
a pin in a stringed instrument (e g a harp or piano) around which the ends of the string are coiled and by which the instrument is tuned

Wurlitzer, Franz Rudolph /'wuhlitsə/
(1831–1900?) German founder of company of mechanical instrument distributors and manufacturers, esp well known for his coin-operated pianos and huge theatre organs

7796679 18/10

X

xylophone /'zielə,fohn/ *n*
a percussion instrument consisting of a series of wooden bars graduated in length and sounded by striking with 2 small wooden hammers – **xylophonist** *n*

Y

yodel[1], jodel /'yohdl/ *vb*
to sing, shout, or call (a tune) by suddenly changing from a natural voice to a falsetto and back – **yodeller** *n*
yodel[2], jodel *n*
a yodelled song, shout, or cry
Ysaÿe, Eugène /i'zie·i/
(1858–1931) Belgian violinist

Z

zapateado /,zahpətay'ahdoh/ *n*
a Latin American dance marked by rhythmic stamping or tapping of the feet
zarzuela /zah'zwaylə/ *n*
a traditional Spanish romantic light opera
ziemlich /'tseemlik/ *adv*
rather
zither /'zidhə/ *n*
a stringed instrument having usu 30 to 40 strings over a shallow horizontal soundboard and played with plectrum and fingers – **zitherist** *n*